The Moral Action: What is it and How is it Motivated?

JOSEF M. SEIFERT

Translated from German by Fritz Wenisch; modified by the author.

Originally published as, *Was ist und was motiviert eine sittliche Handlung?* Salzburg/München: Universitätsverlag Anton Pustet, 1976.

Also available in Polish (*Istota i Motywacja moralnego dzialania.* Opole: Wydawnicto Sw. Krzyza, 1984) and Spanish (*Qué es y qué motiva una acción moral?* Madrid: Centro Universitario Francisco de Vitoria, 1995).

**International Academy
of Philosophy Press**

Irving TX • Gaflei FL
Santiago de Chile • Granada Spain

ISBN: 1540814831
ISBN-13: 978-1540814838

Realist Phenomenological Philosophy: Philosophical Studies of the Dietrich von Hildebrand Chair for Realist Phenomenology at the International Academy for Philosophy — Instituto de Filosofía Edith Stein, Granada.

Realistische phänomenologische Philosophie: Philosophische Studien des Dietrich von Hildebrand Lehrstuhls für realistische Phänomenologie an der Internationalen Akademie für Philosophie — Instituto de Filosofía Edith Stein, Granada

Filosofía Realista Fenomenológica: Investigaciones filosóficas de la Cátedra Dietrich von Hildebrand para fenomenología realista en la Academia Internacional de Filosofía — Instituto de Filosofía Edith Stein, Granada, España.

Volume VI / Band VI / Tomo VI

EDITOR

Professor Josef M. Seifert

EDITORIAL BOARD

Professor Maria Fedoryka (Schoeman), Naples, Fda, USA
Professor Urbano Ferrer, Murcia, Spain
Professor Rodrigo Guerra López, México
Professor Juan-José García Norro, Madrid, Spain
Professor Michael Healy, Steubenville, USA
Professor em. Alice von Hildebrand, New Rochelle,
USA/Belgium
Professor Petro Husak, Vviv, Ukraine
Dr. Hamid Lechab, Austria/Marocco
Professor Feliciana Merino Escalera, Granada, Spain
Professor Jaroslaw Merecki, Rome, Italy/Poland
Dr. Marie Meaney, Italy/Germany/France
Professor Balázs Mezei, Budapest, Hungary
Professor Shahid Mobeen, Rome, Italy/Pakistan
Professor Paulina Monjaraz, Mexico
Professor Emilio Morales de la Barrera, Santiago, Chile
Professor em. Juan-Miguel Palacios, Madrid, Spain
Professor Czesìaw Poråbski, Cracow, Poland
Professor Paola Premoli de Marchi, Milan, Italy
Professor Rogelio Rovira, Madrid, Spain
Dr. Ciril Rütsche, Tübingen, Germany
Professor Stephen D. Schwarz, R.I., USA
Professor Andrzej Szostek, Lublin, Poland
Professor Władysław Strożewski, Cracow, Poland
Professor Mátyás Szalay,
Granada/Spain/Hungary
Dr. Gian Paolo Terravecchia, Padova, Italy
Professor Pedro Jesús Teruel, Valencia, Spain
Professor Cristian Vecchiet, Venice, Italy
Dr. Raquel Vera, Madrid, Spain
Professor Fritz Wenisch, R.I., USA/Austria
Professor Alfred Marek Wierzbicki, Lublin, Poland
Professor Maria Wolter, Gaming, Austria/USA
Professor Wojciech Żełaniec, Gdańsk

DEDICATION

Cordially dedicated to my dear friends Stephen D. Schwarz and Robert Spaemann
In admiration of their excellent ethical writings and in sharing their search for the truth about the Good

ACKNOWLEDGMENTS

Apart from the deep gratitude to my former teachers, most of all Dietrich von Hildebrand and Balduin Schwarz, I wish to express here my profound gratitude to my dear friend Professor Fritz Wenisch, an excellent philosopher himself, who has dedicated tremendous effort and great love to the translation of this work into English, and has helped a lot to make the revised English version of this book better than its German original, and to his dear daughter Magdalena Andres, who has invested many hours and much labor into the formatting and preparing this work for print.

CONTENTS

MOTTO

He who does not want to do good to his fellow man — in such a way that he becomes concerned about the realization of his fellow man's weal — but who merely seizes the opportunity 'to be good,' or 'to do good' in this act, neither is good nor does 'good' ... . The value 'good' ... is located, so to speak, on the back of this act.

M. Scheler

A good will is not good because of what it effects or accomplishes — because of its fitness for attaining some proposed end: it is good ... in itself. ... Even if, by some special disfavour of destiny or by the niggardly endowment of step-motherly nature, this will is entirely lacking in power to carry out its intentions; if by its utmost effort it still accomplishes nothing, and only good will is left (of course ... as the straining of every means so far as they are in our control); even then it would still shine like a jewel for its own sake as something which has its full value in itself. Its usefulness or fruitlessness can neither add to, nor subtract from, this value.

I. Kant

Men of Athens, I am devoted to you, and I love you; but I shall be obedient to the God more than to you.

Socrates (Plato)

Among all natural values, moral values are the highest. Goodness, purity, honesty, truthfulness, and humility of a human are higher than ingenuity, cleverness, a flourishing life, beauty of nature and art, or the well-orderedness and power of a country. What becomes real and lights up in an act of genuine forgiveness, in a magnanimous renunciation, in a burning, selfless love is more important, greater, more significant, and more eternal than all cultural values. The moral values are the focal point of the world; moral disvalues are the greatest evil, worse than suffering, disease, death, or the ruin of flourishing cultures.

D. v. Hildebrand

ABOUT THIS BOOK

The present essay constitutes the English translation, by Prof. Fritz Wenisch, revised by the author, of a significantly expanded version of a public lecture I gave, in January 1975, in the context of my habilitation at the Ludwig-Maximilians-University in Munich.

The primary methods used in what follows for the ethical analyses are intellectual intuitions of necessary essences and insights into states of affairs grounded in these essences as well as arguments built upon the latter.[1]

This method is the foundation of the classical philosophical works, starting with Parmenides, Plato, and Aristotle, up to the present — wherever genuine philosophical results may be found. The method of insight into essences, applied in a systematic way, has, in opposition to the objections raised against it since Kant and Hume, been shown, in the original phenomenological movement within the Munich and Göttingen Circles (through the early E. Husserl, A. Reinach, A. Pfänder, M. Scheler, D. v. Hildebrand, and other thinkers), to be the classical basic method of all genuine philosophizing.

With regard to an explanation and justification of

---

[1] For a more extended discussion of three types of philosophical methods and their subdivisions, many of which are used in this book, see Josef Seifert, *Discours des Méthodes. The Methods of Philosophy and Realist Phenomenology* (Frankfurt: Ontos-Verlag, 2009).

this method, I refer the reader to the fourth chapter of D. v, Hildebrand's *What Is Philosophy?* as well as J. Seifert: *Erkenntnis objektiver Wahrheit.* In the work mentioned last, especially in the "appendix" added to the second edition, the method of insight into essences is elaborated in a critical discussion with transcendental philosophical and neopositivist positions and defended against numerous objections and misunderstandings, such as the suspicion of dogmatism, the charge of an inability to engage in arguments, and the necessity of an irrational and fideist beginning tied to presuppositions, and others.[2]

While empirical-actual motivations can be investigated only through methods such as introspection, depth psychological interpretation of repressed motives, or symbolical interpretive, sociological, and statistical-empirical methods, the philosophical recognition of the intelligible *essence* of the moral action and its motivation which ought to be present — and which makes it into a genuine moral action — is based on the method of the systematically unfolded insight into essences, the method which has just been mentioned.

The reader who does not allow himself to be

---

[2] See also the same author, *Back to Things in Themselves. A Phenomenological Foundation for Classical Realism*, 2nd ed. (London: Routledge, 1987, 2013); *Unbezweifelbare Wahrheitserkenntnis. Jenseits von Skeptizismus und Diktatur des Relativismus* (Mainz: Patrimonium-Verlag, 2015); and Fritz Wenisch, *Die Philosophie und ihre Methode* (Salzburg: A. Pustet, 1976).

convinced of the validity of this method through the attempt of applying it to ethical problems or who, influenced by the current philosophical climate at many universities, takes umbrage at the confidence with which in what follows objective and necessary ethical states of affairs are asserted and, in my view, validly established, I refer to the epistemological works just mentioned and the literature cited in them.

Ethics in the true sense is impossible on the basis of an epistemology which rejects knowledge of objective, necessary structures of essences. For ethics is possible only if the universal essence of moral acts, of their motivation, of an objective ought, and of its sources can be comprehended. Otherwise, one can carry out only a psychological examination of experiences and motives, sociological examinations concerning changes of consciousness, analyses of the ethical language, and similar things. Thus, in the case of thinkers who, following D. Hume, reject any a priori knowledge of essences, such as A. J. Ayer, R. Carnap, M. Schlick, C. L. Stevenson, W. K. Frankena, R. M. Hare, and others, we do not find an ethics in the genuine sense, but a replacement of ethics by the investigations indicated above; wherever such researchers arrive at genuine ethical knowledge or even only formulate specifically ethical theses, this can occur only through leaving behind their own epistemological positions, thus, through presupposing or applying knowledge of intelligible structures of essences of the moral reality which remove themselves as such from purely empirical or language analytical methods of knowledge.

Since the first publication of this work exactly 40 years ago, I have published many other ethical works, the most significant and voluminous one of which deals with the foundations of medical ethics, soon to be followed by a large work on different concrete questions of medical ethics.[3]

University of Dallas, Summer 1975, revised English version, Summer 2016

Josef Seifert

---

[3]   See Josef Seifert, *The Philosophical Diseases of Medicine and Their Cure. Philosophy and Ethics of Medicine.* Vol. 1: Foundations. Philosophy and Medicine, vol. 82 (New York: Springer, 2004). — *Also available as* Kluwer online e-book, 2005.

INTRODUCTION

The question, "What motivates a moral action?" is equivalent with, "What is the essence of a moral action?" For the moral "substance" of an action does not only depend on how the action takes place externally or on the factors objectively connected with it; rather, it depends also on the internal reasons and motives of the action. To give, for example, a large sum of money to the needy is not in itself a generous action; rather, it becomes such an action only because certain motives are present on the part of the agent, or because the realities involved in the objective motivate him in the right way.

The motivation of an action does not only determine decisively *whether* or not an action is morally good; the question of *what* a moral action is also must be answered largely by pointing out what the motive of a moral action is, or what the motive of a moral action *should* be. The question, for example, what factors must motivate an action for it to be morally good, or the question whether humans, when performing moral actions, aim always at their own happiness as their ultimate end such that they remain caught up in themselves in their striving for happiness, or whether humans are, when performing a moral action, capable of a unique transcendence and self-surrender — these questions concern both the motivation as well as the innermost essence of the moral action.

Also, the question concerning the motivation of a moral action can be understood in different ways. One can simply ask what the *actual* motive of a moral action is. This question is primarily empirical and psychological. It belongs to ethics only to the extent to which one asks what the basic *types* of *de facto* motives of moral actions are, and to the extent to which one distinguishes moral from immoral motivations. One can, however, also ask what *should* motivate a moral action, what the motivations are which make a moral action morally good. This question is specifically ethical. The subsequent investigation shall, however, be limited to an "aspect" of this fundamental ethical question. At the same time, many elements concerning the essence of the moral action and going beyond motivation shall be included in the investigation, such as, "What are objective factors of the moral action which, while lying as such outside of the agent's motivation, must nevertheless motivate the agent if he is to act morally?" Related to this, we will ask simultaneously how, in what respects, and in what order of precedence these objective factors must motivate the agent so that we can speak of a moral action. In this sense, we can consider the question, "What motivates a moral action?" as a fundamental question of ethics, a question penetrating deeply into the essence of the moral action. The subsequent essay shall provide a modest contribution to a clarification of this problem.

Before proceeding to answering this question, we must clarify at least briefly the concepts contained in it, or rather the "realities" to which these concepts refer. We can, of course, not present a detailed theory of action and motivation.

1. What is an action?

To start out, I want to note that I use the term "action" only in the sense of one kind of acting freely, and of acting freely in such a way as to realize some state of affairs beyond our act itself. We exclude from our analysis the many forms of creating, procreating, producing, founding, etc. that do not aim at realizing states of affairs but works, things, persons, communities, etc. Distinguishing making (as well as creating/procreating) from acting (doing), we investigate in the following only acting, not free making/creating that shares many characteristics with acting, but differs from it by aiming at bringing into existence (or serving to bring into being) things, beings, persons, communities, etc., instead of just states of affairs: the being (or not being) "a-of-a-B" ("red of a rose").

An action is characterized first of all by its aspect of "reaching beyond itself": Not only does something become real in the acting subject, such as an attitude or a "taking a stand internally"; but an action in the full sense is directed at a state of affairs which is independent of the subject, at the realization of something which is "external" to the agent. This distinguishes an action not only from "taking a stand internally" and from attitudes as such, but also from immanent activities such as running, walking, and others. Also, in order to be able to speak of an action in the true sense, the state of affairs to be realized by the action must be of some significance; moreover, the action must not be merely habitual. Therefore, throwing pebbles into a lake, or rewinding one's watch are not to be called actions, though they realize states of affairs different from the activity itself (the falling of pebbles into a lake, the movement of the hands of my watch); the reason is that either the states of affairs to be realized are too unimportant, or the activity is too habitual and commonplace, or because both are the case simultaneously.

Besides the feature of being "transeunt" (= reaching beyond the acting subject), an action is characterized by the fact that two things are made real in the agent: First, the "taking an internal stand" to a state of affairs, the response to its significance, its importance; second, the act of willing itself, aiming at realizing the state of affairs, an act which exists — in most cases after a preceding act of deliberation[4] — first in the form of a resolve or an intent to carry the action out; subsequently, it achieves, at the proper moment, full reality in the form of those voluntative acts and "commands" which are to initiate the physical and mental activities through which the state of affairs in question is to be realized.[5]

---

[4]   Scholastic philosophy has examined with special care the moments of intention (*intentio*), of deliberation (*consilium*), and others. See Thomas Aquinas, *Summa Theologica*, I-IIae, qq. 12-14. Here, we cannot enter into a more detailed examination of the characteristic features and of the role of these and other elements.

[5]   See on this point D. v. Hildebrand, *Die Idee der sittlichen Handlung*, and above all *Ethics*, pp. 285 ff., 302 ff. There, the dimension of the will as "taking a stand," the first perfection of the will, is carefully distinguished from the (second) perfection of the will as "master" of the action. I recommend for further study above all the investigation of freedom and of the two dimensions of the will carried out there, themes which are only briefly dealt with here. See also Josef Seifert, "In Defense of Free Will: A Critique of Benjamin Libet," *Review of Metaphysics*, Volume LXV, Nr. 2, December 2011, pp. 377-407; "Can Neurological Evidence Refute Free Will? The Failure of a Phenomenological Analysis of Acts in Libet's Denial of 'Positive Free Will'," *Pensamiento. Revista de investigación e información filosófica*, vol. 67, núm. 254, *Ciencia, filosofía y religion. Serie especial no 5* (2011), 1077-1098; and "To Be a Person – To Be Free," in: Zofia J. Zdybicka, et al. (Ed.), *Freedom in Contemporary Culture*. Acts of the V. World Congress of Christian Philosophy. Catholic University of Lublin 20-25 August 1996, Vol I (Lublin: The University Press of the Catholic University of Lublin, 1998), pp. 145-185.
It seems, however, that the second perfection of the will is, above all, confined to actions, and that it is not as unconditionally connected with the first perfection of the will as it is presented in Hildebrand's *Ethics*. He writes, "The term 'will' is not always used

Finally, we find, within the action, the actual realization of the state of affairs, and within the agent, we find a corresponding experience of this realization. Even in cases in which the "willing" to realize the state of affairs is present, this final concluding part of the

---

in the same sense; sometimes it is used in a larger, sometimes in a narrower sense. When used in a larger sense the term 'will' seems to embrace all responses whether volitional or affective. ... When used in the narrower sense it is restricted to the specific act which is at the basis of all actions." *Ethics*, p. 199.

Further, he writes, "The specific character of will" [in the narrower sense] "may be found in its twofold theme: the importance of the object and its coming into existence through our own activity. Thus willing is further distinguished from theoretical responses by the fact that it refers to something which is not yet real (though in principle realizable — and even realizable through me)." (*Ibid.*, p. 201.) In footnote 10 (*ibid.*, p. 201), Hildebrand himself limits this position considerably when he points to acts which he denotes as a "branching out" of the free center rather than as responses in the strict sense (acts such as making something known, promising, obedience, and others), to which, however, he ascribes freedom in the strict sense. In the most decisive passage, though, he writes about the response of the will, "The second perfection, the capacity of intervention in the world around us, is deeply related to the specific inner word of the volitional response. We saw before that only states of affairs [von Hildebrand uses the word "facts" instead of "affairs"] which are as yet unrealized (though realizable) can become the object of our will. We have to add now that the object, in order that we may will it, must be realizable not only in principle but must even present itself as accessible to our own power." (*Ibid.*, p. 286.) To this, it must be responded that in freely "taking a stand," in virtues, or also in free acts of accepting suffering, and in other acts, we can find the first perfection of the will without the will being immediately connected with the second perfection of the will, or without the will being related exclusively to "states of affairs which are not yet realized." See also Footnote 7.

action may be lacking, for it depends always on factors which are not under the exclusive control of the agent, and can be prevented by many purely external circumstances or accidents. As we shall see, this final element of the action — appearing as most decisive from an extra-moral or utilitarian point of view — is irrelevant for the moral value of an action, a fact which all forms of consequentialism fail to recognize.[6]

Closely connected with what has just been said is that, in each action, a state of affairs is presupposed which is not yet realized, and which is characterized by

---

[6] When we use the term "utilitarianism," we are not referring to the mixture of hedonism and utilitarianism which we find in the classical representatives of utilitarianism, such as in J. Bentham, and which J. S. Mill summarizes in *Utilitarianism*, pp. 210 (contained in Volume X of *Collected Works of John Stuart Mill*, edited by J. M. Robson), as follows: "The creed which accepts as the foundation of morals, utility, or the Greatest Happiness Principle, holds that actions are right in proportion as they promote happiness, wrong as they tend to produce the reverse of happiness. By happiness is intended pleasure, and the absence of pain; by unhappiness, pain, and the privation of pleasure." This hedonism, which was held by "classical" utilitarian ethics, is criticized incisively by G. E. Moore in his *Principia Ethica* (see Chapter III), though he entirely shares the decisive principle of utilitarianism — which we could also call "ethics of success" — with the "classical" utilitarians (see the work cited, Chapter V). This principle consists in the view that the moral value and the moral oughtness of an action depends on whether the (total) effects of the action in question are the best ones possible. Thus, the essence of the moral goodness of an act or of an action is shifted into their relation (as means) to positive results (effects). This is how we see the essence of utilitarianism in what follows, as one finds it also in Fletcher's *Situation Ethics*. See J. Fletcher, *Situation Ethics*, pp. 120 ff.

importance [in the sense in which von Hildebrand introduces the term in his *Ethics*, Chapter 1 — translator's note]. We may be directed towards such a state of affairs also in hoping or in wishing; for an action, however, it is also required that the agent has, in his opinion at least, the power to realize the state of affairs. If this is not the case, the act of "willing" the becoming real of the state of affairs cannot even come into existence.[7] Thus, a real or supposed ability on the

---

[7]   D. v. Hildebrand shows this in his ethical investigation of the two perfections of the will (*Ethics*, pp. 284 ff.), especially in his analysis of the manner in which the two perfections of the will are connected (*ibid.*, pp. 286-287). He emphasizes rightly that the willing of something, in the narrower sense of the word at least — that is, at least as a combination and inner unity between a free "taking of a stand of the will" when it is united to the free commanding of an action — can only be directed at still unrealized works (in all forms of making) or to states of affairs not yet real, but realizable through me. To complement and limit what has just been said, I would like to state that the volitional "taking of a stand" (first perfection of the will) may be directed not only at states of affairs, and not only at states of affairs realizable through me. See the previous remarks on making, creating/procreating, and acting. See likewise the examples quoted in Footnote 5. See also Josef Seifert, "Grundhaltung, Tugend und Handlung als ein Grundproblem der Ethik. Würdigung der Entdeckung der sittlichen Grundhaltung durch Dietrich von Hildebrand und kritische Untersuchung der Lehre von der 'Fundamentaloption' innerhalb der 'rein teleologischen' Begründung der Ethik," in: Clemens Breuer (editor), *Ethik der Tugenden. Menschliche Grundhaltungen als unverzichtbarer Bestandteil moralischen Handelns*. Festschrift für Joachim Piegsa zum 70. Geburtstag, pp. 311-360. After the publication of this book in German I had an intense and extended philosophical discussion with Dietrich von Hildebrand in New Rochelle, N.Y., in his home and we arrived at a full agreement that expressed itself in a correction of his position

part of the agent to realize the state of affairs is required for an action to take place.

The following limitation is to be made, however, aiming at precluding misunderstandings concerning the will to realize states of affairs as it is decisive for actions: Within the sphere of actions, we find two basic possibilities, *doing* and *omitting*. Omitting also belongs to the sphere of actions, whether it occurs in the form of a refusal to give in to a temptation, for example, or to submit to blackmail, or whether it consists in simply neglecting to perform an action, or in the refusal to do one's duty. For example, when Socrates refuses to carry out the unjust orders of the government of Athens, as Plato reports in his *Apology*, this explicit refusal to act also belongs to the sphere of "willing to realize," and it is, so to speak, a "negative" will to realize a state of affairs:

> *I, men of Athens, never held any other office in the state, but I was a senator; and it happened that my tribe held the presidency when you wished to judge collectively, not severally, the ten generals who had failed to gather up the*

---

regarding this issue expounded in Chapter 17 of his *Ethics*, 2nd edition (Chicago: Franciscan Herald Press, 1978), and in *Das Wesen der Liebe*; Dietrich von Hildebrand. *Gesammelte Werke* III (Regensburg: J. Habbel, 1971); 2nd Italian-German ed. (Milano: Pompiani, 2003), Chapter 2. Dietrich von Hildebrand explained his change of position in some footnotes in *Moralia*. Nachgelassenes Werk. Gesammelte Werke Band 5, (Regensburg: Josef Habbel, 1980).

slain after the naval battle; this was illegal, as you all agreed afterwards. At that time I was the only one of the prytanes who opposed doing anything contrary to the laws, and although the orators were ready to impeach and arrest me, and though you urged them with shouts to do so, I thought I must run the risk to the end with law and justice on my side, rather than join with you when your wishes were unjust, through fear of imprisonment or death.[8]

These words of Socrates in which he tells us about his conduct lead us to a further question:

2. What is meant by "'moral' action"?

Here, we must begin with the pre-philosophical experience of moral actions. We designate as "moral actions" that part of the totality of human actions which is connected with freedom of the will, responsibility, conscience, merit, and other features; we call those actions moral which we commonly call good, praiseworthy, or noble actions, and which we distinguish from those many human actions to which none of these predicates apply, though they share all the features of an action, such as building, for pragmatic reasons, a new house or a better road.[9]

---

[8]   Plato, *Apology*, 32 b, c. Translated by Harold North Fowler.

[9]   When Moore and Ross emphasized the "indefinable"

16

In this context, we will not take the term "moral action" so broadly as to include the morally good as well as the morally evil action; rather, we intend to limit ourselves to the moral action, that is, to the morally good action, in contrast to the immoral action.

Further, among morally good actions, we will investigate only the essence and the motivation of those actions which we designate as morally obligatory. This is not to suggest in the least that, as asserted by ethical rigorism,[10] all morally good actions are also morally

---

character of the good and the morally good, they saw the character of "good" and "morally good" as irreducible primary data which cannot be reduced to anything else, or which cannot be "defined" through anything else; to attempt this would indeed constitute a "naturalistic fallacy." They overlooked, however, that this irreducibility does in no way preclude a rational insight and an analysis of the essence of value and moral goodness. As a consequence of this confusion, a clear demarcation of moral from extra-moral values is lacking in them, as well as an analysis of the essential characteristics ("definition" of the essence) of the moral and a clear comprehension of value as we can find it within the ethics of value. See D. v. Hildebrand, *Ethics*, Chapters 3 and 15. See also the excellent appreciation and critique of Moore's ethics in Alice v. Hildebrand, "Near-Sightedness of Keen Thinkers — A Critical Study of G. E. Moore," in *Rehabilitierung der Philosophie*, ed. by D. v. Hildebrand (Regensburg: Habbel, 1974), pp. 157-173.

10   See the critique of rigorism in D. v. Hildebrand, *Ethics*, pp. 379 ff. There are, however, also non-rigoristic ethical views which identify — at least according to their intention, but in all likeliness also factually — "morally good" with "morally obligatory," such as the view of Hans-Eduard Hengstenberg. (See Hengstenberg, *Grundlegung der Ethik*, pp. 99 ff.) To begin with, we must agree with Hengstenberg that — within human morality at least — the moral has always a character of an "oughtness" which causes it to be essentially different from all extra-moral actions. Even an

elective morally good action possesses an oughtness in a way completely different from an extra-moral action. Hengstenberg points out rightly (ibid., p. 101) that the person acting morally, even when, for example, saving the life of another, risking his own life, must in all cases subjectively have the sense of having done something that "ought" to have happened, that he could not have just as well omitted.

It seems, however, wrong to assert that every moral action is also objectively obligatory, and further, that subjectively, the agent must have in the moral action not only the sense of doing something that ought to happen, but also something that is obligatory. It belongs objectively to the essence of many moral actions stemming, for example, from magnanimity, from a special compassion, or from a heroic effort, that they are *objectively* not obligatory. It is, above all, essentially connected with love and the moral values proper to it that the loving person does more than what he is obligated to do. This is so not only in the case of the one who is absolutely morally good (divine goodness), but also in a certain respect with humans. On the one hand, the agent (the loving person) may wish to do more for the beloved than what he is morally obligated to, and be clearly conscious of the fact that more is being done; on the other hand, the person for whom the action is carried out will likewise gratefully have this consciousness. He will often thank someone who helps him magnanimously, or does him good, in the *very* consciousness that the other has done something he was not obligated to do, which was, however, morally good nevertheless. Hengstenberg (see *ibid.*, pp. 101-102) paints a caricature of the elective action, of the action which goes, in magnanimity or kindness, beyond what is obligatory. He shifts these types of actions into the light of a complacently condescending conduct which is indeed worthy of being rejected. It is, however, a basic phenomenon within morality that there is — in spite of the unique oughtness even of the freely chosen moral action — still an area of goodness going beyond what is obligatory, an entirely genuine and pure area of heroism, of giving of oneself freely, of magnanimity and kindness with regard to which we do *not* become morally guilty if we omit the action in question. We cannot discuss in more detail the problem of the dividing line between the two kinds of actions. D. v.

obligatory. We acknowledge fully an area of morally

Hildebrand presents in his *Ethics* as well as in his *Moralia* important clarifications. Moreover, Hengstenberg overlooks the experience — in no way offending, but like a moving gift — which provides a special happiness to the person who receives such a good deed which is free in the sense that there is no obligation to perform it. This is a reflection of the primeval religious experience of receiving gifts from God's goodness which are completely undeserved. It is also a primeval experience of a loving person that the beloved bestows, through morally noble attitudes and actions, many gifts on him which are more than what the other was obligated to, which he was not duty-bound to perform, which he did out of the "superabundance" of his love. Though Hengstenberg accepts and clearly expresses his rejection of such an elective area of morality (in this, he falls into the same mistake as Kant to whom he also refers; see *ibid.*, p. 102), and though I consider this as a grave ethical error, he attempts nevertheless impressively to evade the rigoristic consequences of his theory (that we would be obligated in each situation to do what is the most noble in itself, or what is the most noble in this situation). He tries to do this as follows: On the one hand, he expands the area of the obligatory action (on p. 100, for example, he considers saving a life while risking one's own life as obligatory), which constitutes a rigoristic tendency. On the other hand, he asserts, on the basis of his analysis of the "situation" and of the "kairos" for each moral action, that those actions which I see as examples of elective moral actions would, to the extent to which they are not to be subsumed into the expanded area of morally obligatory actions, have no moral value at all, but would constitute a kind of "moral eccentricity." To the extent to which Hengstenberg avoids the rigoristic consequence, he does it at the cost of denying that many morally noble and freely chosen acts have a moral value at all. Thus, he subsumes (in a partial rigorism) one area of morally meritorious and not obligatory actions under the morally obligatory actions; on the other hand (to the extent to which he avoids moral rigorism), he eliminates altogether another large area of moral goodness from the sphere of what is morally good.

good actions which may even constitute the highest part of the world of morality, but which may be freely chosen or omitted without incurring guilt.[11] In this essay, we will confine ourselves to an investigation of morally obligatory actions, not because we wish to limit implicitly moral actions to morally obligatory ones, as has often been done in the history of philosophy,[12] but because we are convinced that the morally obligatory action best exemplifies the essence of the morally good

---

[11]   This is not to say that there are no morally obligatory actions which are also heroic (such as preferring to give up one's life rather than committing an immoral action), and also actions which are among the morally highest (martyrdom, for example) and which are simultaneously morally obligatory. Also, the problem profoundly posed by Hengstenberg in his *Grundlegung der Ethik* will not be dealt with here: What is the extent to which we find in the moral life a process of a "necessitating" through freedom and in freedom, a "necessitating" through which, as I see it, the border of morally obligatory actions may be shifted such that on a higher stage of perfection, many actions may "become" obligatory which were not obligatory on a lower stage? This shifting of the border of morally obligatory actions is presumably derived from obligations (for example, to *continue* commitments one has accepted, and efforts one has engaged in once) which may result from actions which are originally freely chosen and not obligatory. A more detailed analysis of this problem must be omitted here; we cannot even formulate it more precisely. It is only to be emphasized that the difference between morally obligatory actions (the omission of which is culpable) and morally good elective actions is not dissolved on any stage of moral perfection; on the contrary, with greater perfection, the area which goes beyond the obligatory also increases (that is, not only the area of the obligatory actions).

[12]   In Kant's duty-ethics, for example. See notes 10 and 11, as well as the literature cited there.

action such as to exclude misunderstandings. We will prescind from the many problems connected with the area of supererogatory moral actions. The thesis that the morally obligatory action best exemplifies the essence of the moral action does not preclude that for someone, the beauty of moral goodness and certain of its dimensions may come to light as unequivocally or even more clearly in a non-obligatory act of mercy or of magnanimity than in a morally obligatory action. Nevertheless, other essential dimensions of the moral action are given *in themselves* primarily or exclusively in the morally obligatory action; in this action, the philosophical essence of morality comes most clearly to light and can be distinguished most sharply from the extra-moral. This shows itself also in the fact that the moral character of obligatory actions is more universally acknowledged by ethicists, and that, for the most part, it is *subjectively* to be seen more readily than the moral character of actions in which there is no moral obligation. This is ultimately rooted in the fact that objectively, by far the most *important* part of morality, its indispensable core, coincides with the morally obligatory, or rather with the "moral necessity" characterizing it. Only morally *obligatory* actions, responses, and attitudes (virtues) are *indispensably* and *categorically* required of the person. In this sense, we must also qualify the remark that supererogatory moral acts "constitute the highest sphere of morality," or that they may belong to it.

3. What is a "motive"?

In what follows, a "motive" is to be understood as the "why" of our responses and of our will to realize states of affairs or to create some works (for example works of art, communities, states, associations, etc.), albeit a special kind of "why."

First of all, only a recognized or in some way consciously given reason of our willing can be called a "motive."[13] Further, motives of human actions can be objective, that is, they can be situated, on the side of the object, within the state of affairs to be realized. This is so when the suffering of a person who is tortured and unjustly mistreated moves us to come to his aid. We can speak in this sense of motives located on the side of the object (or of objective motives) also when we are concerned with a subjective advantage which is, however, grounded in the object the action is to realize and which motivates us (such as the financial advantage

---

[13]   The question of unconscious motivation cannot be dealt with here in detail. It shall only be emphasized that on the one hand, there are many forms of "unconscious" motives if this is to refer to all those motivations of which the agent does not give a clear account to himself, which he does not recognize as such, which he does not ascertain in reflection, which he cannot name, which are not clearly given to him in lateral consciousness. On the other hand, there is no motivation of which the agent would have *absolutely* no consciousness (in the actual or in the superactual conscious life); for reasons which would lie absolutely beyond consciousness would essentially and necessarily be different from motivation, and with this, also outside of all acting morally. See also A. Pfänder, *Phänomenologie des Wollens – Motive und Motivation*, pp. 152-153.

accruing to a businessman from treating his customers honestly). Motives may, however, also be "subjective" in the sense that the attitudes and dispositions existing within the agent, his love or his envy, his virtues or vices, function as reasons moving his acting. In the following, the important problem of these "subjective" motives and their role for ethics will not or almost not be considered, at least in so far as "subjective motive" refers to special attitudes or individual responses existing in an acting person, and provided that one does not understand the striving for happiness present within each person as a "subjective motive." In what follows, the main emphasis will be on the "objective" motives of actions.[14] We will even mainly investigate realities and factors which are as such entirely independent of the motivation of the acting subject, but

---

[14] In this context, the expressions "subjective" and "objective" are not at all meant to be evaluative, nor are the "objective" motives intended to be presented as less "personal"; in this respect, the terminology I have chosen could be misunderstood. For the sake of simplicity and because of the lack of a better way of expressing matters, the term "objective" is to be understood as follows: It designates all motives of an action which depend on the latter's objective situation (that is, on the situation obtaining independently of different acting subjects) and which are essentially demanded of the acting subject for a fully valid (real) morally good action to come about. "Subjective" is to designate those motives which depend on the individual acting person, and which are to be traced back to attitudes or virtues (or also, in the negative case, to vices or moral imperfections), going beyond the action itself, and not *necessarily* connected with it. A clearer explanation of these concepts would require a more detailed analysis of the various types of motives, which cannot be presented here.

which must motivate an action if it is to be morally good.

Further, a motive is a reason for our acting which does not produce the willing out of itself, and which does not bring the willing about as if it were the cause of the latter (as is the case with the free ego); rather, a motive calls our actions forth in a way similar to an invitation or a challenge. Motives call forth our actions analogously to an invitation which is the reason for our acceptance or for our visit inasmuch as these would not occur without the invitation. Again, similarly as the invitation by itself does not call forth the visit, but only through the appeal to a free act of accepting the invitation, so does the motive call forth an action not out of itself; the motive is a reason for the action only in the sense that it appeals to the free agent to initiate the action freely, that is, it is incumbent on the agent to use that creative self-positing force of freedom, to call into existence that free self-determination and positing of acts to which the motive appeals.

For this reason, a motive is, strictly speaking, not of itself a motive, that is, a ground for acting. Considered from the side of the object, it can be viewed only as a call, an appeal, an invitation, or an obligation to act. It becomes a motive or a reason for our acting only through our free will that allows itself to be moved by the reasons or appeals which come from the object. A motive is, therefore, a reason for our acting only *through freedom*, similarly as an invitation may really be called a reason for a visit, but becomes a reason only through the free act of acceptance.[15]

---

[15] Hengstenberg has seen especially clearly that human motivation stems from freedom. See, for example, Hengstenberg, *Grundlegung der Ethik*, pp. 132 ff. His rejection of determinism — a rejection which corresponds to this concern and with regard to which I entirely agree with him — leads him, however, to the view that the ultimate ground of morality is unmotivated or even *arbitrary*, though he rejects this in principle (see *ibid.*, p. 137). This has its cause in Hengstenberg's lack of understanding of the character of motivation as objective, even if appealing to our freedom (see *ibid.*, pp. 64 ff., 67 ff., 132 ff., 136 ff.), although his analysis of the "attitude appropriate to the logos of things (Sachlichkeit)" [the German word "Sachlichkeit" is used by Hengstenberg as a technical term impossible to translate with a single word or simple expression — translator's note] would open up for him a road to this understanding. According to Hengstenberg, motivation stems, instead of coming from object *and* freedom, in such one-sided a way from freedom that in the final analysis, he lets the moral action flow from a groundless and unmotivated "pre-decision" which is itself not morally good. Instead of seeing how motivation belongs essentially to morality and to its ultimate source (which Hengstenberg identifies as "pre-decision") and how all morally good acting must ultimately be motivated by the objective nature of things and grounded in this nature in order to be morally good, Hengstenberg misunderstands this and explicitly rejects it. This is presumably so above all because he considers it as incompatible with the simultaneous dependence of motivation on the free acceptance of the subject, and because he suspects a determinism where it cannot be found. For the moral action (and all of morality) is essentially "grounded" and motivated by the object *and* at the same time freely called into being by the subject; it is grounded and motivated by the object only *through* the subject's freedom rather than in a "deterministic"-causal fashion. When Hengstenberg calls moral acting — or especially the pre-decision — "groundless," he does not distinguish between five entirely different meanings of "groundlessness": First, by "groundless," one may refer to the essential feature of freedom according to which no free decision can, as flowing from the center of the personality spontaneously

determining itself, sufficiently be explained through an internal or external cause apart from this free center, not even through the objective motive or reason external to the free ego. In this sense, every free decision, every free act is indeed "groundless," a fact which determinism misunderstands. Second, one can refer with "groundless" not simply to all free acts and decisions, but only to those free acts, attitudes, and foundational decisions (Hengstenberg's pre-decision for or against the "attitude appropriate to the logos of things [Sachlichkeit]" belongs here) out of which other free acts and actions grow as from a root without therefore being determined, but also without the arch-freedom and the type of groundlessness of the first free decisions. The latter ones contain on their part the "ground" of the actions growing out of them. These two dimensions of "groundlessness" can be found also in a morally good and obligatory act which is "necessarily" demanded by the object; both of these forms of "groundlessness" are, therefore, even compatible with an object's fully grounding an action, and making it morally necessary. This groundedness consists in the fact that a person will carry out the action with a "necessity" which does not touch the freedom of the action — provided he conforms entirely to truth and to what objectively ought to happen. In this sense we say for example also that God wants the good necessarily and simultaneously freely. Third, one can refer with "groundless" to those free and good actions which are on the one hand grounded and motivated by the object (meaningfully inspired by the state of affairs to be realized, and by its value), but on the other hand, not clearly prescribed, such as all elective free actions (see notes 10 and 11). When confronted with these objects of action, the morally good person can also choose freely; a creation, for example, is free in this sense; the acts referred to here are groundless in the completely new sense that it is left up to the will to decide for or against these actions. In these cases, a person's freedom, his absolutely creative capacity of "positing" spontaneously, of a free "determination" — not prescribed and determined by the object — is *especially mysterious*. While we can say only with regard to the first two meanings of the term "groundless" that the just one wishes to avoid all injustice, we can say with regard to elective actions (or also with regard to divine creation) that the person acts here out of "groundless" freedom in the sense that nothing obligates him or binds him, that there is nothing which makes it *necessary* for him to act in this way. (It is possible, though, that even in the case of elective actions which are clearly motivated by an objective call the element of "groundlessness" referred to here may strongly recede into the background.) Fourth, we may speak of "groundless" actions in an entirely different sense in the case of evil actions, which are also lacking the meaningfully objective element of being directed to and motivated by the importance of the object as we find it in the case of the elective actions. Groundlessness includes here that element of irrationality which stems from a contradiction between the objective importance of an object and the subjective stand of the will. "Groundless" means here that the agent acts against all objective grounds, against all grounds which are truly present. "Groundless" constitutes here a contrast to wisdom, to the wise and prudent action, to acting well; it does, however, not constitute an acting deprived of any understandable motive (jealousy or envy, for example, may be called "groundless" in this sense).

Fifth, we can speak of acting groundlessly when someone acts either senselessly or in an evil way, but "groundlessly" in the sense that there is neither envy nor jealousy, nor any other understandable evil reason which would motivate an unobjective (unsachliche) evil action. "Groundless" in this final sense is Stavrogin's action described by Dostoyevsky in *The Possessed*: Without any reason, Stavrogin bites his uncle in the ear. "Groundless" in this last sense goes hand in hand with "arbitrariness." And *only* actions groundless in this final sense are lacking all motives (at least all objective motives, that is, all motives grounded in the object, as well as those motives which are grounded in a special constitution of the subject; for the motive of wishing to assert oneself through an arbitrary act or a similar motive is present even here). Thus, when Hengstenberg denotes the basic act of morality, the moral arch-decision (pre-decision), as groundless in the sense of unmotivated (and consequently also as not itself moral), he falsifies the essence of the moral act and especially of the morally good act which is or may be "groundless" in the first three meanings of the word, but not at all in the last. It is important for ethics to distinguish most clearly these various meanings of "groundlessness"; and above all, it is important not to confuse the first meaning of "groundlessness," which can even be found in the free act entirely motivated by the object, with "groundlessness" in the sense of arbitrariness and "lacking a motive."

With all that, I believe that in this critical comment on Hengstenberg's view on freedom, I am taking full account of his true intentions, which aim at a complete preservation of free will against determinism. The letter of Hengstenberg's doctrine of freedom, not, however, the spirit of his teaching on the "attitude appropriate to the logos of things (Sachlichkeit)," is contrary to the principle applicable even to arbitrary acts (in the sense of the motive of asserting oneself), and in any case to meaningful and evil actions, a principle the truth of which can be made evident, and which Anselm of Canterbury formulated in *De Veritate* XII as follows: "All willing wills something, and at the same time, it wills because of something. One must, therefore, take into account what a person wills, as well as why he wills it." (Anselm of Canterbury, *Opera Omnia* Vol. I, edited by Franciscus Salesius Schmitt, Stuttgart-Bad Cannstatt, 1968, pp. 193-194.) As this "why" and "because" of *each* willing and of each freely "taking a stand," one may designate the "motive," or the call coming from the object which becomes a motive through the free acceptance.

See A. Pfänder's detailed study *Motive und Motivation*, and especially A. Pfänder, *Phänomenologie des Wollens — Motive und Motivation*, pp. 141 ff. There, he discusses how an act of willing "supports itself" or "grounds itself" in an unique way on a "demand," a "supporting" or "grounding" which makes a potential ground into a real ground of willing. Also, motivation is distinguished from causes and other relations; further, it is shown how motivation *presupposes* "that something which lies outside of the center of the ego is never the phenomenal cause of the carrying out of an act of willing, but always only the center of the ego itself." (*Ibid.*, pp. 148 f.) Of course, if one expands the notion of "causes" from the four Aristotelian "causes" and especially from efficient causality, to other and specifically personal causes, one may describe motivation as a unique and specifically personal cause. See Josef Seifert, *Essere e persona. Verso una fondazione fenomenologica di una metafisica classica e personalistica* (Milano: Vita

Following these introductory explanations, we may now pose the basic question of this essay, the question concerning the essence of the moral action to the extent to which this essence discloses itself through motivation..

---

e Pensiero, 1989), Ch. 9; see also my "Persons and Causes: beyond Aristotle," *Journal of East-West Thought,* Fall Issue Nr. 3 Vol. 2, September 2012, pp. 1-32, and my "Persons, Causes and Free Will: Libet's Topsy-Turvy Idea of the Order of Causes and 'Forgetfulness of the Person'," *Journal of East-West Thought,* Summer Nr. 2 Vol. 4, June 2014, pp. 13-51.

FIRST RESPONSE: THE IMPORTANCE OF THE STATE OF AFFAIRS TO BE REALIZED (THE OBJECT OF THE ACTION)

A first response suggesting itself to the question, "What motivates a morally good action?" is: The state of affairs to be realized, the action's object and its importance motivate the moral action.

Reasons in support of the first response

There are two obvious facts which seem to demonstrate irrefutably that this response is true: First, no moral action is possible having to do with neutral states of affairs, such as with the question on which side of the road a given pebble among thousands of others is located. Since, therefore, a neutral state of affairs cannot ground a moral action, the assumption suggests itself that the special weight, a special importance of certain states of affairs would motivate moral actions.

Second, however, the question of the type of

importance of the state of affairs to be realized — whether it is positive or a negative — obviously plays a decisive role for the difference between morally good and morally evil actions. Any view denying this leads, as M. Scheler has shown, to "monstrous" consequences:

> *Being good and being evil would be entirely independent of all material realization of values. This is indeed what Kant asserts. Whether we attempt to realize what is noble or vile, well-being or suffering, advantage or harm — this would be totally indifferent for the goodness or evil of willing, since the meanings of the words "good" and "evil" would entirely be exhausted by the lawful or unlawful form according to which we supposedly connect the positing of one value content to another.*[16]

---

[16] M. Scheler, *Der Formalismus in der Ethik und die Materiale Wertethik* [*Formalism in Ethics and Non-Formal Ethics of Values* — henceforth referred to as "*Formalism*"], p 46 (passage translated by FW). Kant expresses the view which Scheler ascribes to him here repeatedly, for example, "If the will seeks the law that is to determine it *anywhere else* than in the fitness of its maxims for its own making of universal law — if therefore in going beyond itself it seeks this law in the character of any of its objects — the result is always heteronomy. In that case the will does not give itself the law, but the object does so in virtue of its relation to the will." (*Groundwork of the Metaphysics of Morals*, translated by H. J. Paton, New York, 1964 [henceforth referred to as "*Groundwork*"], p. 108.) As the context shows, Kant is led to the following conclusion, among else because he formulates all kinds of false alternatives (that is, the incorrect opposition of a kind of determination of the

If, however, the content of the value, that is, the respective positive or negative importance of the content of an action, is the determining or in any case the decisive factor of whether we are concerned with a morally good or morally evil action, then it suggests itself to see the motivation through a state of affairs with a positive content as the ground of the morally good action. Solzhenitsyn speaks in the second part of his *The Gulag Archipelago* about the case of a young husband whom the communist authorities suspect, together with his wife, of having anti-Communist attitudes. The husband exculpates himself through denouncing his wife; thus, he causes her to be sent to a concentration camp. In this case, the negative importance of the state of affairs realized (hurt and suffering to his wife, betrayal, etc.) seems obviously to have a decisive influence on the moral evil of the action. When, on the other hand, Socrates intends, as stated above, to avoid the negative state of affairs of an unjust

---

moral act through its object which is indeed destructive of morality over against a will which is entirely and autonomously independent of the nature of the object): "An absolutely good will, whose principle must be a categorical imperative, will therefore, being undetermined in respect of all objects, contain only the *form* of *willing*." (*Groundwork*, p. 112.)

Passages in the text will show that Kant — in contrast to this basic error of formalism in his ethics — at times abandons this false principle of autonomy (which in Kant has still many other meanings which are not distinguished from one another, and which are in part correct, in part incorrect). In the light of such passages, Scheler's objection against Kant would have to be differentiated, although it rightly identifies and rejects a basic tendency of Kant's ethics.

sentencing of the unjustly accused commanders in the sea battle, even to the point of risking his life, it seems, in this case, once again to become unquestionably clear that the importance of the state of affairs the action is to realize — or rather the way in which this importance motivates the agent appropriately or inappropriately — plays a decisive role for the moral value or disvalue of an action.

At this point, however, the question arises immediately as to how the importance of the state of affairs an action is to realize motivates the agent, and how this importance determines the moral value of the action.

Reasons against the first response: Explanation and refutation of what appear to be the only three possibilities of the motivation (determination) of an action by the state of affairs to be realized

There seem to be only three possible responses to this question which shall be examined in what follows.

First possibility: Ethics of success (utilitarianism)

To begin with, the connection between the action and the state of affairs it realizes may be viewed as a means-end relationship. With this, the moral action would be seen as a means and the state of affairs to be realized and characterized by importance as the end of the action. Again, this relationship may simply be understood as objective, taking place outside of the agent's consciousness; or one can consider this means-end relationship as decisive for the agent's motivation: He would intend to reach the state of affairs to be brought about as his real goal, and consider his own action as a means for it. In this case, the moral agent would be led by the question as to what the effect of his action would be. The states of affairs characterized by importance, understood as effects of his action, would constitute the motives of his acting. G. E. Moore summarizes this view, to be designated as "ethics of success," as follows:

> *To ask what kind of actions we ought to perform, or what kind of conduct is right is to ask what effects such action and conduct will produce.*[17]

If, however, one considers this view to its ultimate consequences, one must, in the final analysis, make the moral value of an action dependent not only on the value of the state of affairs which is immediately realized, but also on the (potentially infinite) causal outcomes lying in the future, the value of which would have to surpass that of all alternatives. It follows further from this consequence that there could be no moral obligation for humans:

> *It is obvious that our causal knowledge ... is far too incomplete for us ever to assure*

---

[17]   G. E. Moore, *Principia Ethica*, p. 146.

ourselves of this result. Accordingly it follows
that we never have any reason to suppose that
an action is our duty: we can never be sure
that an action will produce the greatest value
possible.[18]

Refutation of the first possibility

In this success-ethical view, the moral value of an action is degraded to the mere indirect value of a means for reaching a given end.[19] With this, not even the personal

---

[18]   *Ibid.*, p. 149. This utilitarianism in Moore which absolutely passes by the essence of morality is surprising in view of the excellent critical analyses of "naturalist ethics" and hedonism which he carries out in earlier chapters of his work. It is also surprising since Moore comes, in the sixth chapter of the same work, with the principle of "organic unity," very close to the thought of a conduct which is appropriate to things, and which responds to value (a conduct which has nothing to do with mere effects). Regrettably, Moore does not make this thought fruitful for ethics.

[19]   I have offered later a more detailed critique of this view in "Absolute Moral Obligations towards Finite Goods as Foundation of Intrinsically Right and Wrong Actions. A Critique of Consequentialist Teleological Ethics: Destruction of Ethics through Moral Theology?" *Anthropos* 1 (1985), pp. 57-94; "Ontic and Moral Goods and Evils. On the Use and Abuse of Important Ethical Distinctions," *Anthropotes* 2 (Rome 1987); *The Philosophical Diseases of Medicine and Their Cure. Philosophy and Ethics of Medicine.* Vol. 1: Foundations. Philosophy and Medicine, vol. 82 (New York: Springer, 2004) – *Philosophical Diseases of Medicine and Their Cure. Philosophy and Ethics of Medicine.* Vol. 1: Foundations. Philosophy and Medicine, vol. 82, Kluwer online e-book, 2005, Ch. 4-6. "The Splendor of Truth and Intrinsically Immoral Acts I: A Philosophical Defense of the Rejection of Proportionalism and Consequentialism in *Veritatis Splendor,*" *Studia philosophiae*

character of a moral action is taken into account; for if the moral value of an action is to be measured exclusively by the value of the effects, then it is not obvious why events should not have a moral value just like moral actions if these events are caused by circumstances within the non-personal nature, and if they have the same effects as morally good actions (such as the feeding of hungry persons through fishes which happen to swim by, or through influences of the weather on nourishment, etc.). It belongs, however, to the ultimately evident characteristics of moral values that they presuppose a free, personal being. The ethics of success, however, fails to take this fact into account. This view is even much less able to explain the evident difference between moral and immoral means for a good end, and leads inevitably to the false principle that the end would justify the means. Most of all, the ethical view according to which the moral value of an action possesses only an indirect value as a means, entirely borrowed from the value of the state of affairs to be realized (and from its consequences), misunderstands the evident importance which the moral value has in its own right, an importance at which Kant points impressively, and which is entirely independent of the effect accomplished:

Christianae UKSW 51 (2015) 2, pp. 27-67; "The Splendor of Truth and Intrinsically Immoral Acts II: A Philosophical Defense of the Rejection of Proportionalism and Consequentialism in *Veritatis Splendor*," *Studia Philosophiae Christianae* UKSW 51 (2015) 3, pp. 7-37.

A good will is not good because of what it effects or accomplishes — because of its fitness for attaining some proposed end: it is good through its willing alone — that is, good in itself. Considered in itself it is to be esteemed beyond comparison as far higher than anything it could ever bring about ... Even if, by some special disfavour of destiny or by the niggardly endowment of step-motherly nature, this will is entirely lacking in power to carry out its intentions; if by its utmost effort it still accomplishes nothing, and only good will is left (not, admittedly, as a mere wish, but as the straining of every means so far as they are in our control); even then it would still shine like a jewel for its own sake as something which has its full value in itself. Its usefulness or fruitlessness can neither add to, nor subtract from, this value.[20]

---

[20]   I. Kant, *Groundwork*, p. 62. With his thesis that (only) the will is a bearer of moral values, Kant does, on the one hand, not do justice to the metaphysical relation between moral values and the person; for the primary bearer of moral values is the person, not acts, nor the faculty of free will. On the other hand, Kant also suggests a limitation of moral values to the will in the narrower sense, that is, to the will which intervenes through actions. This would, however, neglect the virtues of a person as an independent sphere of moral goodness (and even the most profound sphere), as well as that other area of moral goodness which we find in the case of taking an internal free stand as such. This restriction of morality implicit in Kant's ethics has convincingly been overcome

As Kant shows in this passage, allowing morality to speak for itself, the intention and the disposition of the will to realize a state of affairs guarantees the full moral value of an action, and this value is entirely independent of the success or failure of the action. Thus, the understanding of the relation between the moral action and its object as we find it in the "ethics of success" shows itself to be untenable. Within this conception, not even the elementary distinction between being a mere means for an end and an action being motivated by an end is carried out.

As soon as it is established, however, that the moral value of an action is entirely different from the value an action has as a means for a given purpose, the moral view of the ethics of success shows itself as untenable even if one were to attempt to do justice to the personal character of motivation through the assumption that the value of the action as a *means* for a good end would also have to be an explicit motive of the agent so that an action could be the bearer of moral values. Such a theory would, however, be materially self-contradictory, even apart from the fact that with this "addition," an ethics of success as such would "formally" abandon itself inasmuch as the moral value

by D. v. Hildebrand. See *Die Idee der sittlichen Handlung* and *Ethics*, especially pp. 316 ff. and pp. 342 ff. If, however, the word "will" is used in the same meaning as *free will in whatever form, act or attitude it is present*, then the sphere of morality reaches indeed only as far as the will. Even the noblest feeling of compassion or kindness cannot be morally good if it is not formed or sanctioned by free will.

of an action would have been declared independent of the success as such, and transferred into the motivation. For if the moral value of an action does not depend on the actual success, but on the motivation, or if the moral value is grounded in the will to realize a good as such, then it is impossible to assume at the same time that success as such, of which, as the agent clearly sees, the moral value of the action is independent, would motivate the moral action.

If, however, the moral value of an action does not consist in its indirect value as a means for a positive end, and if it is not the case either that the agent is motivated by the value of the state of affairs to be realized as an end and by the value of the action as a means, how, then, does the importance of an object motivate the moral action?

Second possibility: Hedonism

A second possibility to explain how the motive of a moral action motivates the agent consists in affirming that the driving motive of such an action is the pleasure which the realization of the goal of the action would afford to the agent. According to this hedonistic view, the ultimate motive of all human actions is subjective pleasure, and an action is to be called good to the extent to which it serves this pleasure.

Refutation of the second possibility

Since hedonism is equally affected by the first three

reasons which will be presented below as a refutation of eudemonism, we intend to mention here only two pertinent reasons refuting hedonism. Plato explains them in his *Gorgias*:[21] First, it follows from the hedonistic view that things which are obviously morally neutral would have to be called morally good; if, for example, as Socrates points out, someone scratches his head because he itches and experiences pleasure in doing so, this scratching would, in the eyes of the hedonist, have to be morally good. This is, however, contrary to the evident fact of the moral neutrality of this pleasure and of the activity that causes it. Second, it follows from the hedonistic view that many obviously morally evil actions would have to be designated as morally good as long as someone experiences pleasure in carrying them out. Thus — to remain with the Platonic example — an act of pederasty would be good if only it afforded pleasure to the agent. Likewise, all kinds of crimes which afford sadistic pleasure to the agent would have to be designated as good — an obviously absurd consequence of this view.

Third possibility: Eudemonism

We encounter a third possibility of understanding the relationship between the moral action and its motivating object in eudemonism. This view considers as the driving basic motive of humans not the merely subjective striving for pleasure, but the objective

---

[21]   Plato, *Gorgias*, 494 d ff.

striving for happiness. What the object of the moral action gives to the acting person or what the action itself promises to the agent is not something merely subjectively satisfying for this or that person, but what makes the agent truly happy, the objectively ordered happiness as the fulfillment of the nature of the one acting. The person acting morally is motivated by the state of affairs to be realized through the moral action inasmuch as this state of affairs — in contrast to the action itself and to its consequences — is the source of this happiness. According to this view, the happiness of the agent itself would be the moral agent's exclusive or at least primary motive.

Refutation of the third possibility

There are many reasons which can demonstrate that eudemonism is a moral theory which does not do justice to the nature of the moral action. Here, we will present only five of these reasons:

First, the view that happiness is the reason for acting places the ultimate motives of the morally good action on one level with that of the morally evil action; for on the one hand, the good will is characterized through its being motivated by happiness, and on the other hand, as Aristotle — and with him the great eudemonist medieval ethicists — teaches, all willing would strive inevitably for happiness as its ultimate end.[22] It seems to be impossible to overlook this mistake

---

[22]   See note 25.

after Kant has admirably and clearly uncovered it:

> *The principle of personal happiness is,
> however, the most objectionable, not merely
> because it is false ...; nor merely because it
> contributes nothing whatever towards
> establishing morality, since making a man
> happy is quite different from making him good
> and making him prudent or astute in seeking
> his advantage quite different from making him
> virtuous; but because it bases morality on
> sensuous motives which rather undermine it
> and totally destroy its sublimity, inasmuch as
> the motives of virtue are put in the same class
> as those of vice and we are instructed only to
> become better at calculation, the specific
> difference between virtue and vice being
> completely wiped out.*[23]

Second, as Kant again has shown, in
eudemonism, the categorical imperative of morality is
replaced with a hypothetical one. True, according to the
eudemonist view, human happiness is not a condition
to which moral duties are tied which would depend
only on empirical circumstances, but a condition which
is necessarily met in every human being, at least in the
depth of his soul (this inevitable striving for happiness
is clearly distinct from a consistent, free and conscious
striving for one's true happiness, which few persons

---

[23]   I. Kant, *Groundwork*, p. 109-110.

possess); thus, the hypothetical imperative does not read, "If you want to be happy, then you ought to act in a morally good way" (for humans strive inevitably for their happiness). Nevertheless, however, according to the eudemonist view, the moral demand is made dependent on the condition of striving for happiness which factually is present: Instead of saying, "You ought to do this, you ought to avoid that," instead of being understood in its proper categorical and unconditional character, eudemonism reinterprets the moral obligation into, "Since you want to be happy, you ought to do this, and to avoid that." This presupposes tacitly, "If it would be possible for you not to aim for happiness, all moral demands would cease," or, "If you could become happy in any case, the moral duty would be suspended for you." To deprive the moral obligation in this way of its majestic and unconditional character and to tie it to a condition different from the moral values themselves, making it thereby dependent on a relation which is remote from the moral substance, does not explain the dignity of the categorical-unconditional character of moral demands; rather, it reinterprets the categorical-solemn seriousness of the moral into a hypothetical imperative which is incompatible with the dignity of morality.[24]

---

[24]   See I. Kant, *Groundwork*, pp. 81 ff., and *Critique of Practical Reason*, in Kant, *Critique of Practical Reason and Other Writings in Moral Philosophy*, translated by Lewis White Beck, Chicago, 1949 [henceforth referred to as, "*Practical Reason*"], pp. 146 ff. We reproduce here only what we deem to be evident differences uncovered by Kant; we do not deal with the problematic and

Third, the eudemonist view leads to a virtually immoral consequence with regard to all moral demands connected with our relation to other persons; for the consequence growing out of the eudemonist thesis that one considers other persons as well as intends states of affairs to be realized with regard to these other persons only as means for the goal of one's own happiness (end) is immoral, as once again, Kant has shown thoughtfully. Other persons are always to be respected as ends in themselves or rather for their own sakes; they are never to be used only as means for something else, as means for our happiness, for example. It is unethical to treat them exclusively as means. This becomes most obvious with regard to those duties which relate to the absolute divine person, to the absolutely-personal divine being. Incidentally, at this point, the eudemonist views of the medieval philosophers lead to the strangest and most blatant conflict with the theological views of the same thinkers.[25]

---

erroneous theses which he connected with one of the greatest moral discoveries of all times, the clear distinction between the categorical and hypothetical imperatives.

[25]   Especially in Thomas and the Thomists, we find happiness designated as the final goal of humans, and also as the final motive of human acting which is inescapably pre-given. According to this, humans possess no freedom at all to choose the ultimate goal of their striving, but their freedom is, as Aristotle has asserted already, limited to the choice of means. See Thomas Aquinas, *Summa Theologica*, I IIae, qq. 1-4; 13.

On the other hand, we find in the same thinkers the ultimate goal of creation (and not only objectively, but also subjectively, that is, related to the human will and its motivation) designated as

Fourth, as soon as one has understood the nature of happiness, the eudemonist view leads to an internal contradiction, for it contains a circular argument. According to the very nature of eudemonism, its point of departure is happiness (in contrast to merely subjective pleasure), distinguishing thereby between "true" happiness and mere pleasure. If one wishes, however, to indicate what constitutes true happiness, one will find that it necessarily depends on objective and even moral values, and that with this, it already

---

the *glorificatio Dei externa* (as the glorification of God which creatures are to give). For a presentation of this latter teaching which the Catholic Church has declared a dogma, see M. Premm, *Katholische Glaubenskunde – Ein Lehrbuch der Dogmatik* (4 volumes), Vol. I, pp. 346 ff. (including the literature referred to there). According to this theological doctrine, humans would in the very motivation of the moral action unequivocally be obligated *not* to choose happiness as the ultimate motive of acting (for happiness is a second and subordinate goal of creation); rather, they are obligated to subordinate happiness entirely to the first motive, the glorification of God. In other words, the eudemonist ethics which Thomas takes over from Aristotle stands in a blatant conflict with the theological doctrine on the work of creation, a conflict which is entirely irreconcilable in Thomism.

In contrast, the value ethics presented in what follows is in full harmony with this doctrine, constituting, as it were, its natural philosophical foundation without which this theological teaching must remain philosophically unfounded. With this, however, our ethical view orients itself on the unequivocal ethical data rather than on their relevance for theology. In Thomas, one can find also many other assertions which are contrary to eudemonism. See the excellent presentation of this state of affairs, as well as the respective references to sources, in A. Laun, *Die naturrechtliche Begründung der Ethik in der neueren Katholischen Moraltheologie*, pp. 100 ff.

presupposes moral values, that therefore, it can in no way be their ground. This has been pointed out especially forcefully by M. Scheler and D. v. Hildebrand.[26]

Fifth and finally, eudemonism leads to the assertion that what is morally good is not willed for its own sake, but for the sake of something else. With this consequence, the eudemonist distortion or even undermining of the essence of morality reaches a climax, as Kant vividly expresses:

He affirms that eudemonism tells virtue, *"as it were, ... to her face that we are attached to her, not for her beauty, but only for our own advantage."*[27]

At the end of these considerations, we seem to be faced with an antinomy. On the one hand, the moral experience attests to nothing more clearly than to the fact that a moral action is decisively determined and motivated by the importance of the state of affairs realized through it; on the other hand, none of the forms of the motivation of the moral action through its object that have been discussed above can be supported; and there seems to be no possibility besides the three which have been discussed.[28]

---

[26] See M. Scheler, *Formalism*, pp. 358 ff. We cannot at all go along with Scheler's other theses on the relationship between happiness and morality (his rejection of the idea of retribution, of reward, and others). See also D. v. Hildebrand, *Ethics*, pp. 37 ff., 312 ff., and *The Nature of Love*, pp. 101 ff. and pp. 203 ff.

[27] I. Kant, *Groundwork*, p. 110.

[28] Kant does not distinguish clearly between hedonism and eudemonism. See on this M. Scheler, *Formalism*, pp. 239 ff. Within

Reasons in support of the First Response: Indication and demonstration of a fourth possibility as to how a moral action is motivated by the importance of its object: the object motivates the moral action in virtue of its inherent value and goodness that possess special moral relevance (realization of values, value response, objectivity)

The view of justice as *suum cuique*, which was largely authoritative in antiquity and in the Middle Ages, contains the key for an entirely different understanding of the way in which the object motivates a moral action. We find steps for a clarification of this relationship in Plato, Augustine, Anselm, Thomas Aquinas, Duns Scotus, W. D. Ross, M. Scheler, N. Hartmann, and others; in my view, the most significant contribution for a clarification of this problem can be found in the work of Dietrich v. Hildebrand.[29] It is to be pointed out in this

---

the Thomistic ethics, we find, above all because of the distinction between merely factual and essential nature, a starting point for overcoming of this confusion. On eudemonism within Scholastic and neo-Thomistic ethics and on its criticism, see A. Laun, *op. cit.*, especially pp. 51 ff., 100 ff., and 162 ff.

[29]   I cannot show here in more detail as to how justifications of this "fourth possibility" are present in Plato, above all in the *Gorgias*, but likewise in Plato's doctrine of participation in general, in Augustine in the distinction between two different categories of motivation within "happiness" (Book Ten of the *Confessions*) and in the distinction made in *De Civitate Dei* between the *amor sui usque ad contemptum Dei* and the *amor Dei usque ad contemptum sui*, in Anselm's and Duns Scotus' elaboration of the *bonum honestum*, and in other authors of the great philosophical tradition. Also, we

context, however, that Kant, in stark opposition to his entire formalistic ethics, has seen this fourth possibility concerning the question as to how the object of a moral action can motivate the latter.[30]

> *Suppose, however, there were something whose existence has in itself an absolute value, something which as an end in itself could be a ground of determinate laws; then in it, and in it alone, would there be the ground of a possible categorical imperative — that is, of a practical law. Now I say that man, and in general every rational being, exists as an end*

---

cannot deal here more closely with Scheler's theory that preference should be given to the higher values. All these philosophers have made precious contributions towards the solution of our problem. In my view, however, D. v. Hildebrand has, with his clear distinction between fundamentally different categories of motivation and between morally significant (relevant) and not morally relevant values, accomplished by far the most important contribution to a clarification of this ethical problem of the relationship between the object of an action and the motivation of moral actions. See D. v. Hildebrand, *Ethics*, pp. 34 ff., pp. 257 ff.; A. Laun, *op. cit.*, pp. 126 ff.; F. Wenisch, *Die Objektivität der Werte*; B. Wenisch, *Der Wert. Eine an Dietrich von Hildebrand orientierte Auseinandersetzung mit M. Scheler*; J. Seifert, *Erkenntnis objektiver Wahrheit*, pp. 274 ff.; the same author, "Dietrich von Hildebrands philosophische Entdeckung der 'Wertantwort' und die Grundlegung der Ethik," in *Aletheia. An International Yearbook of Philosophy*, Volume V: *Truth and Value. The Philosophy of Dietrich von Hildebrand*, Josef Seifert ed. (Bern: Peter Lang, 1992), pp. 34-58; and "Wert und Wertantwort. Hildebrands Beitrag zur Ethik," in *Prima Philosophia*, Sonderheft 1, 1990.

[30] See note 16. See also I. Kant, *Practical Reason*, pp. 170 ff.

in himself, not merely as a means ... All the
objects of inclination have only a conditioned
value; for if there were not these inclinations
and the needs grounded on them, their objects
would be valueless.

Persons, however, are, as Kant points out, objective ends the existence of which is an end in itself; thus,

in its place we can put no other end to which
they should serve simply as means; for unless
this is so, nothing at all of absolute value
would be found anywhere. But if all value
were conditioned — that is, contingent —
then no supreme practical principle could be
found for reason at all.[31]

Here, Kant points at a kind of being motivated by an object which differs completely from the ones discussed so far. This motive motivates the agent not only or primarily through his own happiness, let alone through the mere subjective pleasure which the object affords; rather, he is motivated by the importance the object has in itself, by its "absolute value." This "absolute" — which means here objectively grounded in the being itself — value, its intrinsic preciousness belonging to this being, is, as Kant emphasizes, the

---

[31]   I. Kant, *Groundwork*, pp. 95-96. The translation by Paton used here omits the word "practical"; the corresponding word ("praktisches") is, however, contained in the German original.

ultimate source without which reason could find "no supreme practical principle ... at all." In the moral action, therefore, the agent gives to the object of the action what "belongs to it," what is "due to it."[32]

Although this role of the object of our motivation is in no way confined to values which are objective and which stand in themselves — or rather to the bearers of such values[33] — it is nevertheless the case that the moral

---

[32] Kant occasionally touches upon this due relation, already recognized in the classical idea of *suum cuique* as the essence of justice, in his statements about respect, but in no way does he acknowledge it in its basic metaphysical and moral importance. In D. v. Hildebrand, on the other hand, we find an explicit recognition and detailed analysis of this relation. See D. v. Hildebrand, *Ethics*, pp. 191 ff., pp. 244 ff. H.-E. Hengstenberg comes close to a conception of this relation in his teaching on the role of "Sachlichkeit" (attitude appropriate to the logos of things) within morality. See his *Grundlegung der Ethik*, pp. 33 ff.

[33] Thus, the metaphysically limited situation of humans is also a source of moral obligations. Similarly as a child may not claim the rights of the parents or a citizen the rights of a king because objectively, they do not possess these rights, so may humans not arrogate divine rights to themselves. This source of moral obligation prohibits suicide, euthanasia, and artificial birth control. See on this point J. Seifert, "The Problem of the Moral Significance of Human Fertility and Birth Control Methods. Philosophical Arguments against Contraception?" in *Humanae Vitae: 20 Anni Dopo*, Acts of the Second International Congress of Moral Theology, Rome, 1988, pp. 661-672. "Una reflexion filosófica y una defensa de *Humanae Vitae*. El don del amor y de la nueva vida," in: Benedicto XVI, Karol Wojtyła, Carlo Caffarra, Antonio María Rouco Varela, Angelo Scola, Livio Melina, Alfonso López Trujillo, Fernando Chomali, Josef Seifert, *A cuarenta años de la Encíclica Humanae Vitae, Cuaderno Humanitas* No 19, Pontificia Universidad Católica de Chile, Octubre 2008, pp. 49-59. Rights, commitments freely entered into (such as promises), objective

obligation finds its most original foundation in being inasmuch as it is the bearer of absolute (Kant) or objective (Hildebrand) values. With this, it is in no way necessary to consider these values as "entities"

---

goods for a person, and others, also are sources of moral obligations which cannot be reduced to values. (In this respect, D. v. Hildebrand's work *Moralia*, mentioned already, has presented further explanations and some additions to his *Ethics* which is too exclusively founded on morally relevant values. See v. Hildebrand, *Ethik*, pp. 290-292, note 79. [This note can be found only in the German edition of *Ethics* as it has been included in the *Gesammelte Werke*. Translator's note.]) H. Reiner, in his books *Die philosophische Ethik* (pp. 216-217) and *Pflicht und Neigung* (pp. 143 ff.), exemplifies the fact that even literature specialized in ethics ignores the category of motivation through the objective "good for the person" which D. v. Hildebrand has introduced into ethics in addition to the "important in itself" (goods which carry value) and the "merely subjectively satisfying." In his criticism of D. v. Hildebrand's ethics, he ignores the latter's most important contributions made since the 1930s, especially the elaboration of the "role of the 'objective good for the person' within morality." See D. v. Hildebrand, *Die Menschheit am Scheideweg*, pp. 61 ff., *Ethics*, pp. 393 ff. In these books, H. Reiner's positive concern is taken into account in a much more differentiated way; at the same time, the objectivity of values is fully elaborated without having to embrace the "compromise" between value ethics and hedonism which H. Reiner suggests (see H. Reiner, *Die philosophische Ethik*, p. 217), a compromise which cannot convince in the least, and which threatens to lose sight of the basic metaphysical-ethical datum of value.

See also Josef Seifert, "Dietrich von Hildebrand on Benevolence in Love and Friendship: A Masterful Contribution to Perennial Philosophy," in *Journal of Philosophical Inquiry and Discussion: Selected Papers on the Philosophy of Dietrich von Hildebrand, Quaestiones Disputatae* 3, no. 2 (Spring 2013): 85–106. Also audio/video registration http://www.hildebrandlegacy.org/main.cfm?r1=7.50&r2=1.00&r3=1.00&r4=0.00&id=109&level=3.

separated from being, as neo-Kantianism, Rickert, N. Hartmann, or also Kelsen understand them (each of them in a different way).[34] Rather, values constitute the "core of being," they are being itself inasmuch as it is important or precious in itself.[35]

This basic thought allows one to achieve the decisive ethical breakthrough concerning our problem. We avoid the Scylla of hedonism and eudemonism as well as the Charybdis of ethics of success and utilitarianism. Inasmuch as the object of an action "demands" our moral action, and inasmuch as we give in this action the response due to a being, the importance of the object of our action, of the state of affairs to be realized, is indeed what motivates us in our acting morally; but it motivates us neither through

---

[34] See the criticism of this view presented by the following authors: F. Wenisch, *Die Objektivität der Werte*; B. Wenisch, *Der Wert*; W. Waldstein, "Vorpositive Ordnungselemente im römischen Recht," *Salzburger Universitätsreden*, H. 19, 1967. See also note 35.

[35] Concerning this, see J. Seifert, "Die verschiedenen Bedeutungen von 'Sein.' D. v. Hildebrand als Metaphysiker und M. Heideggers Vorwurf der Seinsvergessenheit," in *Wahrheit, Wert, und Sein*, edited by B. Schwarz; the same author, "Being and Value. Thoughts on the Reform of the Metaphysics of Good within Value Philosophy" in *Aletheia* I, 2 (1977) (German and English). Here, we cannot deal with the history of the philosophical discovery of value as given evidently and objectively, a history taking its point of departure above all in F. Brentano's important work, *The Origin of our Knowledge of Right and Wrong*. More often than not, such a central distinction is lacking from the ethics of value. An example is H. Reiner. See his book *Die philosophische Ethik*, pp. 217-218.

subjective pleasure, nor primarily through the true happiness it affords us, but rather through its preciousness resting in itself and through its plenitude of value. Our willing/acting is due to this preciousness. At the same time, on the one hand, the object clearly motivates us such that the will is a response adequate to the object of the action, an "internal stand appropriate to the logos of this object";[36] but on the other hand, the value of the willing is entirely independent of the success or the usefulness of our action. For the value of a response which is due to a good remains entirely unaffected even if no success is granted to this willing. The will to realize a state of affairs which is at the basis of a moral action as well as the "taking of a stand" which make this will possible do not receive their moral values from the success to which they would have to be subservient like means; rather, they receive their moral value from their "inner rightness"[37] through which they are the response due to the being in question, and through which they fulfill an objective metaphysical "due-relationship."[38] This makes entirely clear that, as Kant emphasizes, the moral action to which success is denied also keeps its full moral value and still shines

---

[36] A "sachliche Stellungnahme" (translator's note). See H.-E. Hengstenberg, *Grundlegung der Ethik*, pp. 33 ff.

[37] Unfortunately, we cannot deal here with the philosophy of value response in terms of the inner rightness of the moral act, a view which has been developed especially by Augustine, Anselm, and Bonaventure.

[38] See note 32.

like a jewel for itself, "as something which has its full value in itself."[39]

As D. v. Hildebrand has shown in a pioneering way, a further distinction would have to complement the rational justification of the moral value of an action at which the above considerations have arrived. Those bearers of values, such as a talent for playing chess or soccer, which, while calling for appreciation and admiration, do not ground moral demands or obligations, must be distinguished from the bearers of morally relevant values. Human life, for example, possesses a morally relevant value, for not only does it issue, like the chess genius of Steinitz or Magnus, a general extra-moral call for being appropriately appreciated, but it grounds those specifically moral demands and duties which appeal, in their unique seriousness, to our conscience.[40]

In this context, the question whether there are other sources of moral obligation besides the value of a being, such as rights, obligations freely entered into, the metaphysical limitations of humans, and similar ones is not decisive;[41] for a convincing proof of the first answer to the question of what motivates a moral action has succeeded at one point. There are beings to which our acting based on willing is due because of their morally relevant values; the values which some beings bear (the

---

[39] See note 20 and p. 37.

[40] See D. v. Hildebrand, *Ethics*, pp. 57 ff.

[41] See note 33.

human person or human life, for example) are such that they make our intervention through acting even morally obligatory. If we witness an attack on an innocent person's life and are able to help, the objective and morally relevant value of this human life makes our action obligatory. If we contemplate the characteristics of human beings and their personal dignity which is grounded, among else, in their power to know, their freedom, and their destiny, we recognize this morally relevant value immediately through a most rational insight.[42]

Serious objections against the sufficiency of the first response

We must not complacently acquiesce in this first response to our question; rather, we must examine further whether the question as to what motivates a moral action has been answered sufficiently. This examination is required above all because significant objections may be raised against the just explained manner in which the moral action is motivated by its object; especially two objections seem to make the truth of the first response to our question again dubious.

First, often, the moral value of an action is evidently higher and more "absolute" than the value of the state of affairs to be realized through the action. To

---

[42]   Concerning the problem of insight into essences see J. Seifert, *Erkenntnis objektiver Wahrheit,* pp. 129 ff. and the literature referred to there.

begin with, this is true in the simple sense that, from the standpoint of value, the moral value of a life-saving action "enriches" the world much more, realizes a much higher value, than the mere fact that a human being stays alive.[43] Similarly, through murder and the moral guilt connected with it, a much deeper disharmony comes into the world than through the death of a human. Moral values and disvalues are the most "absolute," the highest values and the worst disvalues within the naturally given universe.[44] This shows itself still more clearly when one considers another sense of

---

[43] This self-evident truth can be understood when one contemplates the incomparable superiority of the values made real through free acts, their meritoriousness and others of their characteristics, and when one compares them with the value of human life which lacks all these moments. In another respect, however, a human life, which constitutes the basis of many moral acts, is metaphysically not strictly comparable with the value of a single moral act.

[44] With regard to moral disvalues, this can again be made fully evident when one compares an extra-moral evil with a moral one. To stay with our example, a human's death is a great evil; but as such, it is not freely caused, the terrible disharmony of guilt and of conscience is not present, God is not offended or rejected through this death (see pp. 40 ff.). Thus, in Dostoevsky's *Crime and Punishment*, for example, the death of the old usurer which appears even desirable to Raskolnikov certainly does not constitute as profound and absolute an evil as the moral evil connected with Raskolnikov's action of murder. Overlooking the independence and superiority of what is morally good and evil over all extra-moral goods and evils constitutes one of the basic errors of utilitarianism, of situation ethics (especially in the form in which Fletcher presents it) and of many other erroneous ethical views.

the "absoluteness" of moral values to which Kant points at the beginning of his *Foundations of a Metaphysics of Morals*. Moral values alone are to be called "absolute" and to be praised without restriction in the sense that they, as long as they remain moral values and are not motives for immoral actions or attitudes, are not only valuable in a certain respect, but absolutely. [45]

> *It is impossible to conceive anything at all in the world, or even out of it, which can be taken as good without qualification, except a good will. Intelligence, wit, judgment, and any*

---

[45] See Josef Seifert, "Moral Goodness Alone Is 'Good Without Qualifications': A Phenomenological Interpretation and Critical Development of some Kantian and Platonic Ethical Insights into Moral Facts which Contribute to the Moral Education of Humanity," in *The Paideia Project* (20th World Congress of Philosophy in Boston August 10-15, 1998) http://www.bu.edu/wcp/Papers/TEth/TEthSeif.htm. In the passage now following, Kant does not consider the fact that Pharisaism feeds not only on imaginary, but also on real moral values. Moral values can, therefore, become a great moral danger and lead to a Pharisaic pride much worse than moral faults growing from other passions. It is, however, true that Pharisaism destroys precisely the moral value of the person — at least of his present moral acts. In this sense, one can say that the moral value cannot enter into the service of evils as long as the value remains present. As long as a moral value exists, it remains present in its splendor of value; unlike a magnificent talent, it can never become "absorbed" into the service of an evil, and become itself "evil." We cannot enter here into the question in which way the moral values of past moral actions remain present although they provide nourishment to Pharisaism; nor can we discuss the question of what the various ways are in which goods can enter "into the service" of evils.

other talents of the mind we may care to name, or courage, resolution, and constancy of purpose, as qualities of temperament are without doubt good and desirable in many respects; but they can also be extremely bad and hurtful when the will is not good which has to make use of these gifts of nature, and which for this reason has the term 'character' applied to its peculiar quality. It is exactly the same with gifts of fortune. Power, wealth, honour, even health and that complete well-being and contentment with one's state which goes by the name of 'happiness', produce boldness, and as a consequence often over-boldness as well, unless a good will is present. ... Moderation in affections and passions, self-control and sober reflection are not only good in many respects: they may even seem to constitute part of the inner worth of a person. Yet they are far from being properly described as good without qualification (however unconditionally they have been commended by the ancients). For without the principles of a good will they may become exceedingly bad; and the very coolness of a scoundrel makes him, not merely more dangerous, but also immediately more abominable in our eyes than we should have taken him to be without it.[46]

---

[46]   I. Kant, *Groundwork*, pp. 61/2. With this passage, Kant

Kant emphasizes rightly that only moral values are "absolute" in the sense that without them, other goods in a person such as a keen intellect would be evils, while these values are good in themselves and by virtue of their most proper essence. How, then, is it possible, however, that much lower and less "absolute," morally relevant, goods, such as health, life, happiness — goods which to support is morally good and obligatory — can motivate a moral action? It seems impossible that the moral action which is good in a much more absolute sense is motivated by a good much less "absolute" such as health, animal life, or even human life.

In response to this difficulty, one could point out with Thomas Aquinas, for example, that a personal act such as knowledge or also the will receives its value not exclusively from its object, but also from the subject, from the person. Thus, knowledge about all beings lower than humans has a higher value than these beings themselves.[47]

---

enforces at least a radical revision of the so-called cardinal virtues. These can be called "virtues" exclusively inasmuch as they participate in the morally good and value-responding qualities of other virtues. This holds true at least of prudence, fortitude, and temperance. They are morally good exclusively if they are prudent moral goodness, courageous moral goodness, and temperate moral goodness or love. Justice, on the other hand, is essentially an elementary moral virtue. We must forego in this context a more detailed critical analysis of the cardinal virtues.

[47] Once again, this can be recognized when one makes present to oneself the essential superiority with regard to values of the personal, consciously-awakened free being over the non-personal

Even so, knowledge remains fully directed to these beings as its objects, though the latter are, from the point of view of value, below humans. Thus, also a free voluntary act supporting life and health possesses, as a personal act, a higher value than health and life themselves, but it still remains motivated by these morally relevant goods.

Doubtlessly, this response contains a profound truth which illuminates the dignity of the personal-spiritual being. Nevertheless, this answer to the difficulty mentioned does not seem to be sufficient. In any case, it seems that the inner grandeur and the unique nobility of moral actions prohibit seeing their *only* motive in goods such as life, health, and others, even when the moral action is directed towards these goods, and however weighty these goods may be.

This still unresolved difficulty is increased considerably through a second objection against the sufficiency of the first response to the question concerning the motivation of a moral action: If one investigates more carefully the *datum* of a moral action, it turns out clearly that the (morally relevant) value of the state of affairs to be realized is not exclusively its motive. For the moral agent clearly wills the object of a moral action not as unconditionally as he wills to fulfill a moral obligation. In experience, this becomes obvious especially in the case of the avoidance of an immoral

---

being. Then, it becomes obvious that an act of knowledge in which we grasp the truth about a stone or an animal has a higher value than its object.

action. If we are ordered to murder an innocent person, being threatened that otherwise our own lives and that of our families will be destroyed, we are obligated not to act; we ought to have an unconditional will not to carry this immoral action out. As much as this will ought to be co-motivated by the innocent person's morally relevant value and depend on it (we could kill a dog, for example, in such a situation), as little do we will the good of the innocent person's life more unconditionally than the lives of our family and of ourselves. On the contrary, our family's life is justifiably more important to us than the innocent person's life. Quite obviously, therefore, the motive for which we do not kill him and for which we rather let our family perish is not such an unconditional interest in the object of the action — the innocent person's life; rather, one must look for an additional motive of the moral action in order to explain this "unconditional interest" of the person acting morally. Further, our practical lives would be entirely unbearable, even literally "impossible" if our interest in the morally relevant goods with which moral obligations are connected (such as life, health, etc.) in the "objects of our action" would be as *unconditional* as the interest we have in such "unconditional" a way in acting morally, and obeying the voice of our moral conscience, in which we have an "absolute" interest. The fact that the morally relevant value of the state of affairs to be realized by an action cannot be the exclusive motive for our acting morally becomes especially clear if we think of the sacrifices which we are to undergo in order to realize a morally obligatory action or omission, and if we compare these sacrifices with those which we would take upon ourselves for the sake of the realization of the state of affairs to be brought about through the action. While we would have to be ready to risk our lives rather than to disregard a moral obligation through our acting, or even to be ready to sacrifice the lives of many, indeed of all humans, rather than to commit an injustice, it would be absurd to assert that we would be prepared to undergo similar sacrifices for the sake of the object-value as such (such as an innocent person's life whom we are asked to murder) in which a moral obligation is grounded. Thus, it is impossible for us to be interested in the value of the state of affairs to be realized to such an extent that it would explain the unconditional interest characterizing the moral action. The (morally relevant) value of the object of an action can, therefore, not be the only motive of the moral action. This becomes most obvious if we think of examples in which we would not undergo any sacrifice for the sake of the value of the object of a moral action. Normally, it certainly is a part of the moral action that we should be ready to undergo certain sacrifices (entirely independently of the question of the moral obligation) only for the sake of the value of the state of affairs to be realized (for example, for the sake of the value of an innocent child falling into the water or also for a child about to be aborted). In other more rare cases of morally obligatory actions, however, we need not have any interest in the action's object as such; we may even wish that it would not exist. If, for example, after World War II, Hitler would, as a private person, have been drowning and we would have been able to help him without risking our lives, we would have been obligated to save his life. Similarly, we are obligated to omit the action of euthanasia in the case of a dying cancer patient who feels excruciating pain.

In both instances, it is entirely permitted not only not to undergo any sacrifices for the sake of the respective state of affairs as such which is to be realized through the action, but even to wish or hope that its opposite might be the case and that Hitler or a gravely suffering person might die.

These instances show most clearly that it is impossible for the value of the state of affairs to be realized through an action to be a sufficient motive for a moral agent's unconditional interest, and that the moral action does not simply constitute an adequate response to the value of the object and the state of affairs to be saved or realized through our action.

Once again, we are confronted with a seemingly insurmountable difficulty, a seeming antinomy. On the one hand, it is clearly given that the importance of the state of affairs to be realized through a moral action has a decisive impact on the moral action and its motivation; on the other hand, the specific nature of the moral action itself does not seem to allow viewing the moral action as being motivated by the value of the state of affairs realized through the action (which certainly not always and not exclusively, and never completely, explains the full weight of our moral obligation).

A solution to this difficulty is to be searched for in the following direction: On the one hand, the object of the moral action and the importance of this object play a decisive role for the moral action and its motivation; on the other hand, this object is not the sole and sufficient motive of the moral action. The truth of this thesis will become clear through an examination of further answers to the question as to what the motive of a moral action is.

SECOND RESPONSE:
THE MORAL DUTY AS SUCH MOTIVATES
THE MORAL ACTION

A more in-depth analysis of the moral action shows that in it, there is something differing from the subject as well as from the object of the action: the moral obligation, which is characterized by the following features:[48] First, it is entirely objective, that is, it is

---

[48]   In his *Ethics*, D. v. Hildebrand does not explicitly recognize, as an entity in its own right, the moral obligation (duty) confronting the moral agent from the side of the object. (See *Ethics*, pp. 257 ff.) There, he considers as the main (or exclusive) motives of the moral action on the one hand the value of the good on the side of the object, on the other hand the moral value of one's own action. In *Morality and Situation Ethics*, pp. 63 ff., D. v. Hildebrand exhaustively investigates the "moral obligation," and introduces the important distinction between "formal" and "material" obligation. Connected with this, attention is called to the moral obligation as a *new* moment over against the morally relevant good, even if not as an "entity in its own right" in the sense to be explained; for the moral obligation is primarily understood as a demand to give the response which is due to the morally relevant good. See *op. cit.*, pp. 131-132.

independent of the wishes and inclinations of the agent. This objectivity of the moral obligation possesses an "unbendingness of reality" equal in rank to that of the object of the action. The moral duty possesses, in some respects, an even higher reality and objectivity, going beyond that of the object of the action. This is so on the one hand because of the majesty of the moral duty, on the other hand because of the fact that a moral obligation may be present even in the case of unsuccessful actions. Second, however, it must be stated with respect to the reality of the moral obligation that it

---

Hildebrand does not present the moral obligation as something demanding a response that goes beyond the response to the morally relevant object as such, as something that demands its own response which is, in most cases, precisely *not* due to the object of the moral action. As a second motive of the moral action, only the moral value of one's own action is elaborated in this work, similarly as in his *Ethics*. It is suggested that moral consciousness consists mostly or exclusively in the response to this value. In my view, this is the reason why Hildebrand must carefully differentiate moral consciousness from a false or Pharisaic self-reflection: as a not wrongly self-conscious interest in the moral value of one's own action. As pertinent as these explanations are, it remains nevertheless true that one can determine the nature of moral consciousness, independently of this difficulty, through the fact that the person acting in a morally conscious way apprehends not only the value on the side of the object and responds to it, but that he apprehends also the entirely new reality of the moral obligation and responds to it. This obligation presents itself to him also as located on the side of the object, and as a moment entirely different from the good in which it has its origin. See also the following explanations in the text. This is not to deny that moral consciousness *also* includes the interest in the moral value of one's own action; rather, this will presently be explained in more detail.

depends on the reality of the subject as well as on the situation and state of affairs to be realized through the action (that is, on the object of the action). More accurately, the existence of a moral duty depends on the encounter between the subject and the morally relevant object as well as on certain factors of the situation brought about by this encounter.

We should never forget an important truth about human action. Even if, in the human action in the strict sense, the will has a state of affairs as its immediate object, the acting person does not respond primarily to the value of a state of affairs. And even if he cannot bring about a person through his action of saving his life, he responds primarily to the value of the person and to the person himself whom he saves and not to the value of the state of affairs that he be saved.

The moral obligation comes into existence through the encounter of a person and a morally relevant object, and it comes into existence as a consequence of this encounter. Neither the object as such (a drowning person, for example), nor the subject as such (the rescuing person considered in himself) are grounds or bearers of the moral obligation, nor does the moral obligation exist in the object or in the subject of the moral action as long as they are considered in themselves. Rather, this obligation comes into existence only when the subject (the potential rescuer, for example) consciously encounters the object (the drowning person for example) in a concrete situation, or when he recognizes the object consciously.[49] For an obligation to exist at all, a person must recognize the object from which the moral obligation proceeds. Third, even after this encounter has occurred, the moral obligation does exist neither "in" the subject nor "in" the object of the action, but, so to speak, "above" and "between" both. It does, however, constitute itself not at all as an "aspect" or "appearance" of an object for a subject, similar to the various forms of appearances and perspectives. The moral obligation does exist in no way only as an entity which would be constituted merely by persons or by "intersubjectivity" and community.[50] It

---

[49]   Subject and object may, however, coincide, as is the case with all moral obligations concerning one's own person (true self-respect and true self-love, as well as all morally obligatory actions or omissions which are a consequence of the two and which relate to one's own life, health, bodily and spiritual integrity, development, purity, and other matters).

Moreover, there are — only or primarily outside of the sphere of action, to be sure — moral obligations relating to attitudes and virtues, obligations which are entirely independent of a particular situation and which are always present.

[50]   Today, it is especially important to emphasize this since many forms of ethical immanentism or relativism teach exactly the view criticized above.

Even if a moral duty relates to a community or to other persons, it is as little a merely subjective "positing" of this community as is the metaphysical being of these persons themselves. Concerning the objectivity of knowledge and especially of the knowledge of values, see J. Seifert, *Erkenntnis objektiver Wahrheit*, as well as the literature referred to there. The realities which are elaborated there (pp. 140 ff.) as existing "in themselves" also include the moral obligation which is quite real in itself in the sense indicated there. See also Josef Seifert, *Back to Things in Themselves. A Phenomenological Foundation for Classical*

possesses an incomparably higher and more objective form of reality; it is present "in itself" between and "above" the agent and the object of the action. It also has the character of "breaking in from above," like a call coming from the outside, like a "spiritual" call, but with this, incomparably more real than any call coming from a human being because of its objective binding force from which the agent can be dispensed neither through himself, nor through the human being to whom the action is directed. Indeed, if we prescind from indirect forms of dispensation,[51] no being at all can change the essence of this obligation; it possesses a character which is independent of human or divine discretion.

While the moral obligation shares this last mentioned feature (its independence of any person's will) with laws of ideal essences,[52] it differs from them through a fourth feature: The moral obligation is in no way an abstract entity, something ideal, a universal plan of essences; rather, the moral duty contains a

---

Realism (London: Routledge, 1987, 2013).

[51] Such an indirect dispensation occurs, for example, if an authority suspends a positive command or if a person to whom we have made a promise foregoes the fulfillment of what has been promised. See A. Reinach's excellent examination on the promise in "The A priori Foundations of the Civil Law," translated by John F. Crosby, in *Aletheia — An International Journal of Philosophy*, Vol. III (1983), pp 28 ff.

[52] See on this J. Seifert, *Erkenntnis objektiver Wahrheit*, pp. 266 ff., and by the same author, "Bonaventuras Interpretation der augustinischen These vom notwendigen Sein der Wahrheit", *Franziskanische Studien* 59 (1977), pp. 38-52.

unique synthesis between historical concreteness directed to the agent "here and now," and universality inasmuch as it would be directed in the same way to any human being in the same situation, and "eternity" inasmuch as it demands, in its fatefulness, a decision "in" time, not, however, "for" time, but for eternity. This may be the reason why Kierkegaard calls the moral obligation the "breath of the eternal."[53] Connected with this concrete character with which the moral obligation directs itself to the agent — as well as with the second and third feature of the moral duty identified above — is the fact that it possesses an *addressee* to whom it is issued. This addressee is, however, the respective *individual* person who is in the given situation and simultaneously (in contrast to a social act such as a promise) not one or more definite persons, but all persons who would be, under every point of view, in the same situation. Moreover, unlike what happens in the case of a social act, a promise, for example, the moral obligation does not proceed from an "addresser's" freely chosen spontaneous act. The moral obligation does, at least with regard to how it is given, not at all proceed from a person. We will later deal with the fact that the moral obligation also has, in an entirely different way, its ultimate metaphysical origin in an

---

[53] S. Kierkegaard, *Concluding Unscientific Postscripts to Philosophical Fragments*, Vol. I, edited and translated by Howard V. Hong and Edna H. Hong, Princeton, 1992 [henceforth referred to as *Postscripts*], p. 152. See also Kierkegaard's subsequent expositions on the relation of morality to eternity.

(absolute) personal being, and "proceeds" in a certain way from this being. This relationship is, however, fundamentally different from the one obtaining between a social act and the person performing it (the addresser); also, the moral obligation is unequivocally given as such before one understands any relation of it to its ultimate personal foundation of being.

Fifth, the moral duty is characterized by a seriousness, an unbendingness, and an absolute character of "oughtness" which the object of the moral action and the value of the object in no way possess in almost all cases of moral actions.

One can see this when one considers a further (sixth) feature of the moral obligation: It demands a unique response. Strictly speaking, to be sure, one cannot say that an adequate response is "due" to the moral obligation, for, unlike, say, a person, it is not a being bearing a value. One must state, however, that the moral duty demands a unique response of obedience, of an absolute submission which cannot be understood at all as a response due to the *object* of the action. This kind of unconditional submission is not demanded by the preciousness of the drowning person, whom we owe sympathy, love, and so on, but it is demanded only by this specifically moral obligation.[54] Later, we will return

---

[54]   M. Scheler explicitly denies this object or motive of the moral action. See M. Scheler, *Formalism*, pp. 191 ff. Scheler considers "duty" as essentially opposed to one's own "inclination"; he even construes an opposition between "duty" and "one's own willing," as if someone could no longer do out of duty what he truly "wills himself." Finally, Scheler sees the element of duty as contrary to a

to its ultimate metaphysical foundation.

Kant points this out with these words: *"Duty is the necessity to act out of reverence for the law. For an object as the effect of my proposed action I can ... never [have] reverence."*[55]

It would indeed be a significant mistake in ethics to overlook the fundamental difference between the moral obligation and the object of the moral action, as

---

moral action which flows from one's own ethical insight. Scheler sees correctly, to be sure, that to be able to speak of duty presupposes a contingent being which is *capable* of moral evil. It would be absurd to speak of divine duties, even though one can speak with full right of divine goodness. As soon as a finite being exists, however, the element of being obligated is a positive datum which is not at all opposed to one's own willing or to one's own insight. It seems that we find in Scheler at this point more a reaction against the Kantian ethos rather than a phenomenological analysis of the essence of the moral obligation. All one needs to think of is the experience of Florestan which Beethoven has expressed artistically in his Fidelio ("Sweet, sweet comfort in my heart: I have done my duty!") in order to see how thoroughly compatible full insight and joyful acting are with the consciousness of a moral obligation. Indeed, at the basis of moral obligations, such as the obligation not to lie or to act justly (in contrast to supererogatory moral actions), is even a metaphysically-unique "necessary oughtness" which manifests itself in humans as a consciousness of duty, in God as an impossibility to act differently. The absoluteness of the duty not to lie or to judge unjustly is, on the contingent level, a mirror of the absolute necessity that an absolutely good divine person can never judge unjustly or lie. The response to this "necessary oughtness" (duty) can *only* be free (an unfree being could never respond to such an "oughtness"); it constitutes even a fulfillment of the highest meaning of freedom.

55   I. Kant, *Groundwork*, p. 68.

well as that between the two kinds of "taking a stand" corresponding to each of these two elements. It would, however, be an even more serious ethical mistake — a mistake which Kant commits in the basic thoughts of his ethics[56] — to deny that the moral obligation in most cases (except in cases of purely positive commands) depends strictly on the importance of the state of affairs to be realized although the obligation is, in most cases of moral actions,[57] "emancipated" from this state of affairs or rather although it constitutes, in relation to this state of affairs, an entirely new element. Even so, the moral obligation depends, in a narrower and in a wider sense, on the nature of the object of our act and of the state of affairs to be brought about.[58] In the case of a

---

[56] See note 16.

[57] This does not apply to all moral actions, inasmuch as moral actions are possible in which the adequate response to their objects and the response to the moral obligation coincide in the sense that the moral obligation does not demand the "taking of a stand," but consists in giving to the object of the moral action the response that object demands. This is, for example, the case with some actions which relate to moral values (for instance with the obligation to avoid an occasion of moral evil, or also with religious duties relating to God).

[58] A moral obligation depends in the full sense on a state of affairs to be realized when the moral relevance characterizing the state of affairs according to its essence is the ground of the moral obligation (for example, in the case of saving a human life, preventing an immoral act, etc.). The moral obligation depends only in a wider sense on a state of affairs to be realized in those cases in which a state of affairs becomes important only "from the outside," for instance through a promise or a positive command. In these cases, the state of affairs is made obligatory only because of its property of being "something promised" or "something

completely neutral state of affairs, it is impossible that there could ever be a moral duty to realize it. Thus, the existence of a duty depends on the importance of the state of affairs to be realized. Moreover, the rank and the weight of the moral obligation to act depends strictly on the nature, the rank, and the weight of the state of affairs to be realized, not, however, in the sense that a state of affairs characterized by a higher importance would always automatically include a weightier and more unconditional obligation to realize the state of affairs, but in the sense that the importance and the nature of the state of affairs in question always strictly determine the *kind* of the moral obligation relating to this state of affairs. If, for example, the *health* of one patient who does not suffer from a life-threatening disease and another's *life* are at stake, the higher and "more urgent" importance of the life (as constituting the basic ground of all other personal goods) demands that it be saved first if the other circumstances of the two situations are equal. Again, a very minor evil (insignificant pain) on the part of another does not impose an unconditional obligation on a person noticing the pain through encountering the one suffering to attempt to alleviate this pain even if he has the power to do so. In the case of great pain, however, such a duty is unquestionably imposed on him. It shows itself equally clearly that in the case of negative actions, the gravity of the importance of the

---

prohibited."

object (the "matter") of the action is decisive for the degree of the immorality of the action: For example, deceiving another with regard to an insignificant good for him (a small business gain) is immoral to a much lesser degree than deceiving him with regard to a high good for him (for example, with regard to his wife's love for him, as we find it in Shakespeare's *Othello*, where Iago deceives Othello and alleges his wife's unfaithfulness). In a word, the rank of the value, the gravity of the importance of a good for a person, its urgency and other factors of the importance of the object in question strictly determine the existence, the nature, the degree, and the urgency of a moral obligation. Consequently, intending to separate the moral obligation from its object, as Kant clearly attempts it in his ethical formalism,[59] is a radical mistake contradicting the most evident states of affairs of ethics.

Moreover, important as it is to acknowledge with Kant that the moral obligation demands a *unique* response (respect) and submission, it is equally important to acknowledge simultaneously that precisely the moral obligation also demands of the agent to give the response due to the importance of the state of affairs to be realized. It would be downright immoral and consequently not a fulfillment of our moral duty if we were interested *exclusively* in fulfilling it and not at all in the realization of the state of affairs to

---

[59]   See note 16.

be brought about for the sake of the importance characterizing it. One may, to be sure, concede to Kant that an exclusive interest in the morally relevant good on the side of the object (an alleviation of suffering, for example), as many ethical views propagate today, does not ground a real moral action — at least in most cases.[60] Using Kant's terminology and insight, one could speak here of an action which is, while being according to duty (being objectively in accordance with the moral obligation), not an action "from duty," that is, an action which is also motivated by following the moral duty. Moreover, this moral obligation — a recognition of which has nothing to do with "legalism" or an "ethics of law," but is a basic datum of the moral sphere — directs itself at the person in an original way, takes him incomparably seriously, and does not at all constitute a depersonalizing abstract legality.[61] A

---

[60]   In some cases, such an "exclusive" interest in the object of the action without an interest in the moral value of one's own acting is impossible. This applies, for example, to all actions which aim at the coming about of moral values or at the avoidance of moral disvalues, as well as to the will to avoid a situation seducing one to moral evils. See note 77.

[61]   This is how situation ethicists present the moral obligation. See the elaboration of the character of morality as being totally directed at the person in D. v. Hildebrand, *The Nature of Love*, p, 206: "On the one hand, we have here a high-point of transcendence in the pure commitment to the morally relevant value. But on the other hand, this call, insofar as it is morally obligatory, pre-eminently contains the element of *'tua res agitur'* ('your personal concern is at stake'). In a certain sense this call is my most intimate and personal concern, in which I experience the uniqueness of my self. Supreme objectivity and supreme

subjectivity interpenetrate here."

It is paradoxical that especially situation ethics and the type of utilitarianism which goes — particularly in Fletcher — for the most part hand in hand with it and which wishes to do away with absolute obligations, is anti-personalistic. This shows itself also in Hegel's reinterpretation of ethics — akin to utilitarianism — into his view to be termed "world-historical" situation ethics according to which the value of an individual action consists in its effectiveness in world history. Kierkegaard brings out masterfully the anti-personalistic effect of any philosophy of this kind as well as the absolutely personal character of the moral obligation in his *Postscripts*: "Ethically, what makes the deed the individual's own is the intention, but this is precisely what is not included in world history, for here it is the world-historical intention that matters. World-historically, I see the effect; ethically, I see the intention. But when I ethically see the intention and understand the ethical, I also see that every effect is infinitely indifferent, that what the effect was is a matter of indifference, but then of course I do not see the world-historical." (p. 155.) "World-historically, one does not see the individual's guilt such as it is only in the intention, but one sees the external deed consumed by the totality and in this totality sees it bringing upon itself the consequence of the deed. Therefore he sees something that ethically is altogether confusing and nonsensical, sees that the well-intentioned deed brings down upon itself the same consequence as the ill-intentioned deed — the best of kings and a tyrant occasion the same calamity. ... He sees something that ethically is an offense, namely, that world-historically he must ultimately disregard the true distinction between good and evil, since this is only in the individual, and in each individual actually only in his relationship with God." (p. 156.)

Especially in his emphasis on "becoming a subject as highest task," Kierkegaard highlights how the ultimate self, the completely individual person, awakens when confronted with the absoluteness of a moral demand. It is not to be denied that Kierkegaard, because of his equivocal use of the term "subjective," in some passages places into question the objectivity of the factors motivating the moral act; in this way, he himself shows tendencies of situation ethics. In our view, however, this aspect of unique response corresponds to this moral duty as such; and only an action which indeed takes place also "for the sake of this duty," out of "obedience" to this duty, can be designated as an action "from duty" and can, provided that a moral obligation is present,[62] be the bearer of a full moral value.

If one sees, however, that the action is *not exclusively* "from duty," but is motivated *also* by the fact that the agent is giving the response due to the importance of the state of affairs to be realized and to the person loved and affirmed in his action, then the fact that the action takes place "from duty" receives a character entirely different from the isolated and thereby distorted way in which Kant presents it. Thus, what is at stake is an organic interpenetration of the first and the second motive of the moral action that were discussed. To use an example, in the case of a moral duty to correct a state of affairs which we have incorrectly presented and to inform another person of a truth decisive for his well-being, we ought to be concerned about the fulfillment of the moral duty; but simultaneously, we ought also to be genuinely concerned about the fact that the state of affairs be communicated, and that the truth be known by the other. Moreover, we fulfill our obligation only if we are also truly concerned about the realization of the state of

---

Kierkegaard does in no way affect his innermost ethical concern.

[62] As we have seen, there are also actions which are morally good without being obligatory. See notes 10 and 11.

affairs characterized by an importance from which the obligation indeed proceeds. Only from this point can the elementary givenness of a hierarchy of obligations — which is entirely ununderstandable, given Kant's starting point — also be explained; as things stand, the original datum of the moral obligation itself can become understandable only on the basis of this ethical insight, while it cannot at all be explained merely on the basis of a criterion of a general and non-contradictory maxim of acting, a maxim which is present also in morally neutral cases.

One could object to such a theory of a double or complex motivation of the moral action that it would teach a multiplicity of motivation instead of a unity, and that this is unphilosophical. We will investigate the groundlessness of such an objection, and the fact that only reality can decide whether recognizing several principles or only one principle for the explanation of something is the more "philosophical" attitude.[63]

---

[63]   W. D. Ross emphasized this masterfully in his discussion of hedonistic utilitarianism. See W. D. Ross, *Foundation of Ethics*, pp. 82-83: "The view which admits only one intuition — that only the production of maximum good is right — gratifies our natural wish to reach unity and simplicity in our moral theory. We have a natural wish to reach a single principle from which the rightness or wrongness of all actions can be deduced. But it is more important that a theory be true than that it be simple; and I have tried to show that a system which admits only this one intuition is false to what we all really think about what makes acts right or wrong. ... It is, to my mind, a mistake in principle to think that there is any presumption in favour of the truth of a monistic against a pluralistic theory in morals, or, for that matter, in metaphysics either. When we are faced with two or more

Naturally, the following important ethical question arises at this point: How do the two motives of the moral action which have been analyzed so far relate to each other, and which one of them has priority?

Generally, one can reply to this question that the response to the importance of the object has priority insofar as the moral obligation itself is grounded in this object, depends in its content on this object, and can be known only through a recognition of the importance of this object; also, the obligation is related to this object. On the other hand, the motive in the sense that the action occurs "from duty" has priority inasmuch as it is present in all morally obligatory actions, and inasmuch as it demands a special absolute submission which is not to be refused even for the sake of a purpose which

---

ostensible grounds of rightness, it is proper to examine them to find whether they have a single character in common; but if we cannot find one we have no reason to assume that our failure is due to the weakness of our thought and not to the nature of the facts. Just so in metaphysics; where we find two types of entity that are prima facie quite different, as bodies and minds are, it is proper to ask whether they are not two forms of one kind of entity; but there is no reason for assuming that they necessarily are; and if on examination we can find no unity of nature in them, it is wiser to accept this result than to assume that there must be a unity that we have not discovered. There is no reason why all the substances in the world should be modifications of a single pattern." With regard to the analogy of the ultimate metaphysical difference between spirit and matter (soul and body) which is irreducible to a unity, see J. Seifert: *Leib und Seele*, pp. 3 ff.; pp. 170 ff.; pp. 189 ff., and *What is Life? On the Originality, Irreducibility and Value of Life*. Value Inquiry Book Series (VIBS), ed. by Robert Ginsberg, vol. 51/Central European Value Studies (CEVS), ed. by H. G. Callaway (Amsterdam: Rodopi, 1997).

may be ever so lofty, while in many cases of moral actions the state of affairs realized does not at all demand a similar submission. In some cases, we may even wish that the state of affairs which we realize might not even obtain, or that the state of affairs which is not to be realized by us (such as a suffering person's liberation from his pain through death) might obtain. This question would have to be investigated through considering one by one all possible cases of obligatory actions, and then, two things would clearly show themselves: On the one hand, the submission to the moral duty has in *all* cases priority for our motivation, or rather, it should have priority. As long as there is a moral duty, and as long as it is not "superseded" in a given situation by a higher and more urgent duty (such as the duty to live up to an agreement which is superseded by the higher and more urgent duty to save a life), we must not disobey a moral obligation, even if we could, through this disobedience, bring about a moral value which is much higher than that of our own action — something which is impossible in itself. At this point, moral reality and utilitarianism contradict each other most flagrantly. Whatever consequences may follow our actions, whichever state of affairs on the side of the object may be realized, we must give in *all* cases priority to the moral duty addressing us; for it addresses the individual in a deeply personal way as a *"tua res agitur,"* and I would not be permitted to disobey it even in the imaginary case in which through disobeying a moral duty something more valuable in itself would come about on the side of the object.[64] This shows clearly the motivational priority which the obedience to the moral duty is to have in all cases of morally obligatory actions, as can clearly be known through an insight into the intelligible essence of the moral.

On the other hand, there are cases in which we should, in a *certain* way, be concerned more with the object of our moral action than with the fulfillment of our duty as such. I say "in a certain way," for this is not at all contrary to the priority which the moral obligation always is to have in motivation — a priority which has just been emphasized. In the sphere of action, I ought, in all cases, to obey this obligation "primarily." If, however, one refers with "being motivated" to the exclusively internal "taking a stand" of the will to the degree with which one affirms something in its being and gives an assent of the will to it,[65] to the sanctioned

---

[64] As mentioned already, this holds true even for the fictional situation that we could prevent, as the effect of a morally evil action, a greater *moral* evil or bring about a moral good. This shows that the unique "absoluteness" of the moral obligation stems not only from the fact that the moral disvalue exceeds by far all extra-moral evils, but also from the fact that the moral obligation commands and addresses the person "in all circumstances" and "regardless of all effects." It points out to the agent that his actions have an "ultimate" weight of their own, a weight so absolute that it can never be regarded as a means for other ends; rather, the goodness and evil proper to his actions must be considered in complete disregard of possible effects. This throws a deeper light on the "absoluteness" of morality which has been explained on p. 21 (and notes 45 and 46).

[65] This is the first perfection of the will inasmuch as is not

joy and love[66] or to a wishing, then the moral agent should in many cases allow himself to be motivated more by the state of affairs to be realized; in this case, he would do an injustice if he would in this sense be interested "most of all" in fulfilling his moral duty. Even if we prescind in this context from the motivation of the responses accompanying the action and also from the influence which indirect freedom has on them,[67] we must here nevertheless distinguish between the internal response of the agent's will and the element of the action which has earlier been designated as the will to realize the respective state of affairs. And on the basis of this distinction, we can say that the internal response of the agent's will should in some cases and in a certain way allow itself to be motivated more deeply by the object to be realized than by the obligation as such. In such cases, the inner response of the agent should direct itself in a certain way more at the state of affairs to be realized and the person or good to which it is related than at the obedience to the duty as such; and if this would not be the case, the agent would even act immorally. The clearest case of this is the religious

---

restricted to the sphere of action. See notes 5 and 7.

[66] See D. v. Hildebrand, *Ethics*, pp. 316 ff. There, it is demonstrated that affective responses such as joy or love also can become bearers of moral values if they are sanctioned by the free will (through the use of cooperative freedom). The analysis of "cooperative freedom" and of its central role within morality belongs to the most significant contributions which D. v. Hildebrand has made to ethics.

[67] See note 66.

action, for example, the action of a Catholic priest who says mass, believing in the Catholic doctrine (this example is understandable also for someone who does not agree with the Catholic faith, but who nevertheless understands the moral duties which someone sharing this faith does objectively have; for the moral duty obtains even with regard to merely supposed states of affairs).[68] This priest must, in fulfilling his duty to say mass on a Sunday,[69] be concerned infinitely more with the objective event as well as with the superior value which it serves than with fulfilling his duty as such. In the sphere of action he must, to be sure, always give priority to duty; but since in this case, the value of the state of affairs to be realized is superior to the moral value of his own action, this superiority should also have the effect of a certain priority of motivation of the response to the value of this state of affairs. The state of affairs which in itself is more significant is also, in a certain way, "more to be willed" by us. This can also be understood through examples of natural morality. When we seek, for instance, to avert a great moral evil (murder or adultery, for example) through a simple word of advice which we are duty-bound to give, we

---

[68]   This is in no way to suggest that the Catholic doctrine on holy mass concerns states of affairs which are only supposed. With faith in the truth of the Catholic doctrine concerning the Sacrifice of the Mass revealed by God, I appeal, however, as an ethicist also to the ethical understanding of those who do not share this faith.

[69]   He is not necessarily subject to this duty, but it can be present because of certain factors (such as obedience).

should, in the characteristic sense, be concerned more with the coming about of the state of affairs to be realized than with fulfilling our duty as such; and the response to the gravity of the importance of the state of affairs to be realized should have a certain priority, not at all affecting the different priority of the moral duty, at least with regard to our inner response of the will which is at the basis of our acting.

At this point, it may seem that the uncovering of two different factors for the motivation of the moral action and the explanation of the relation they have to each other have answered sufficiently the question concerning this motivation. Our examination of further answers to this question will, however, show that this is mistaken.

THIRD RESPONSE:
THE MORAL VALUE OF AN ACTION IS SIMULTANEOUSLY THE MOTIVE OF THE ACTION

A detailed investigation of the moral action shows that it seems at least as if the moral value inherent in a moral action also would motivate this action: Neither does the object of the moral action necessarily have a moral value,[70] nor does the moral obligation as such ever have a moral value. The moral goodness of an act is, however, a unique perfection of this act, a perfection which has the following incomparable predicates: Only a person can be its bearer, it is rooted in free will, it implies responsibility, conscience, merit, and it is

---

[70] Often, the morally relevant state of affairs an action is to realize is an extra-moral one, even if the action is morally good. This is the case, for example, when physical or spiritual suffering is alleviated, a life is saved, and in similar instances. In other cases, the morally relevant value on the side of the object is itself a moral one, such as in the case of an effort aiming at preserving the moral purity of a child.

deserving of a reward. The uniquely praiseworthy plenitude of the value of a moral act can, in the case of many moral actions, in no way be found in the states of affairs to be realized (the life of a drowning person, for example, has no moral value whatsoever); also, the moral obligation itself is never praiseworthy, meritorious, or a bearer of other moral predicates.[71]

Many everyday expressions bring to light or suggest that this unique value of the moral action as such also plays a role in the motivation of a moral action. Thus, someone may perhaps say that he wishes to be good, that he wishes to become better and morally more perfect; and many a person may say or think that he wishes to do good, to get rid of his moral faults, and so on. This is also expressed in the basic principle recognized by traditional philosophy, a principle which has been considered as the first and most evident of all moral principles: "What is good ought to be done, what is evil ought to be avoided."[72]

---

[71] This moral obligation continues to be present even in the case of the morally evil action and condemns the latter, as in the case of murder, for example. In this case, we may, therefore, speak very well of a moral obligation (just as in the case of a good action), but not of moral goodness.

[72] See Thomas Aquinas, *De Veritate*, q. 16a. 1, 2, especially a. 2, resp.; see also *Summa Theologica*, I-IIae, q. 94 a. 2. To be sure, in this context, a clear distinction between the *moral* goodness of an act and the morally *relevant* goodness of the object of a moral action (such as the education of children or the return of a borrowed object) is missing in Scholastic philosophy. We can use the formulation of this basic moral principle in our context only to the extent to which it refers to what is *morally* good and evil as such.

D. v. Hildebrand introduces the moral value as a new and decisive basic motive of morality; he sees the difference between the "morally unconscious" person — who does not realize the full moral value — and the "morally conscious person" precisely grounded in the fact that the former is concerned with the value of the state of affairs to be realized, but not with the moral value of his own act, while the morally conscious person is also motivated by the moral value of his own act.[73]

Contrary to this, Max Scheler completely rejects this motive of the moral action:

> *But Kant is correct on one point. It is in essence impossible for the value-contents of "good" and "evil" themselves to be the contents of a realizing act ("willing"). For instance, he who does not want to do good to his fellow man — in such a way that he becomes concerned about the realization of his fellow man's weal — but who merely seizes*

See also my article, "¿Qué es la ley natural? Su reforma y renovación personalista y axiológica con algunas observaciones críticas sobre su fundación aristotélica-tomista y eudemonista," Quién, revista de filosofía personalista de la Asociación Española de Personalismo, N°. 3, 2016, págs. 7-22.

[73] D. v. Hildebrand, *Ethics*, pp. 257 ff. There, it is shown how the general will to be morally good as well as being motivated by the moral weight of one's own intervention indeed are "value responses" which are neither Pharisaic nor wrongly self-regarding, and which belong essentially to moral consciousness. See also note 48.

the opportunity "to be good," or "to do good"
in this act, neither is good nor does "good"; he
is truly an example of a Pharisee who wishes
only to appear "good" to himself. The value
"good" ... is located, so to speak, on the back of
this act, and this by way of essential necessity;
it can therefore never be intended in this act.[74]

Scheler sees here, to be sure, that the moral agent's interest in the value of the state of affairs to be realized is decisive, and that an isolated interest in the moral value of one's own act (without an interest in bringing about the well-being of one's neighbor, for example) may even destroy this moral value. In this sense, the moral value of an action does indeed appear "on the back" of the action.

One must also agree with Scheler that Pharisaism essentially implies isolating an interest in one's "own goodness" from all concern for the good to be realized. (Pharisaism implies, to be sure, an even much deeper perversion and an ungenuine interest in the moral value of one's own action.[75])

Nevertheless, the Scheler quotation contains the following theses which are both mistaken and contrary to the nature of the motivation of moral actions: First,

---

[74]   M. Scheler, *Formalism*, p. 27.

[75]   That is, the interest in the moral values of one's actions stands in the service of one's own greatness, of the pleasure in one's own greatness, and of self-glorification. See D. v. Hildebrand's analysis of the Pharisee in *Ethics*, pp. 445 ff. See also the literature referred to in note 31.

Scheler asserts, implicitly at least, that any isolated interest in one's own goodness is Pharisaic. As D. v. Hildebrand's analysis of other self-regarding attitudes has shown, however, this is not the case: There is a forced and scrupulous concern with the goodness of one's own acts which lacks all features specific of Pharisaism.[76] Second, Scheler affirms, implicitly at least, the thesis that an interest in the moral value of one's own act includes necessarily a lack of interest in the object. Most of all, however, our quotation from Scheler explicitly asserts that the value "morally good" can "never be intended in this act." This seems to deny apodictically that a moral act can be motivated by the moral value the action brings about. This is, however, clearly false, as D. v. Hildebrand has demonstrated convincingly:[77] First of all, an agent does not at all have to intend the moral value of his own action necessarily or primarily[78] in a reflexive way as something that

---

[76] See D. v. Hildebrand, *Ethics*, pp. 261 ff.

[77] See D. v. Hildebrand, *Ethics*, pp. 259 ff.

[78] A certain consciousness of one's own moral values does not destroy them. This is demonstrated by Socrates as Plato depicts him in the *Apology*, by Paul, who says of himself, "I have fought the good fight...," and many others, inasmuch as we find here a non-Pharisaic consciousness of one's own moral values. It is true, however, that, in accordance with the individual response to oneself, the consciousness of the moral "task" to be realized must always have the prevailing weight. The consciousness to be the bearer of moral values is still very different in Socrates' and Paul's case. In the case of the latter, it is connected with the humble conviction that in the final analysis, everything that is good in us is ultimately to be ascribed to divine grace with which we can

"adorns" him; rather, he may consider it as an objective "task," as something "to be realized" by him. This does not even necessarily include reflection, let alone a false self-reflection or Pharisaism, as Scheler asserts. On the contrary, the perception of the call to realize moral values contains a special objectivity and subordination of the moral agent. This is so because these values are characterized by a unique objectivity and majesty; and in addition, the moral agent's awareness of the call to realize these moral values goes hand in hand with a singularly special humility which could never be grounded in the mere realization of the object and which is motivated by the consciousness of how little the moral agent measures up to this task. Further, the interest in the moral value of one's own action is not at all necessarily a Pharisaic "circling around oneself" and self-glorifying; rather, it is a value-responding "taking a stand"[79] in which the moral value is intended for the sake of its inner preciousness with respect to which, as mentioned before, it surpasses by far all extra-moral values of states of affairs to be realized. It would be a decidedly unethical attitude not to will the much higher moral value of one's own intervention (in the case of saving a life, for example), and to intend only the value

---

only freely cooperate; thus, Paul experiences that our moral "ability" also has the character of a gift which humans would not have from themselves or as standing in the slavery of sin. These elements are absent in the case of Socrates, at least in this explicit form.

[79]   See the literature referred to in note 76.

of the human life on the side of the object.

This becomes clearest in the religious motivation of the supernatural action. Here, we aim at realizing moral values in us directly as a glorification of God, in the case of a Christian, as a way to become similar to Christ, and every trace of a wrongly self-regarding attitude disappears from being motivated by the moral value of one's own intervention.

Even apart from the religious motivation of a moral action, though, there is, already on the level of natural morality and its experientially accessible structure, nothing perverted in being motivated by the moral value of one's own intervention which is thematic here. Anselm of Canterbury points this out sharply, even with a one-sided emphasis:

> *The just one who intends what ought to be preserves, to the extent to which he is to be called just, the rightness of the willing because of this rightness, not because of anything else.*[80]

This moral value of willing what ought to be and of being motivated by the inner rightness of the willing must fully be recognized as a decisive moment of moral consciousness.

In relation to the other two motives of the moral action, this motive follows the others in a certain

---

[80] Anselm of Canterbury, *De Veritate*, 12, p. 194. "Therefore, that will is just which preserves its rightness because of this rightness itself." *Ibid.*

temporal and logical order: For first, the morally relevant importance of the state of affairs to be realized and the moral obligation grounded in it must be comprehended so that the moral value of one's own morally obligatory acting can be understood at all.

On the other hand, one may say in general: Being motivated by the moral value of the intervention — a motivation ultimately inseparable from an understanding of the moral obligation and the response to it, and immediately following this understanding — need not be consciously experienced as clearly as being motivated by the moral obligation. The former "shares," however, with the latter the same priority characterized above with respect to the being motivated by the importance of the state of affairs to be realized.

It holds likewise true of the internal response of the will that it should, in some cases of moral actions described above — as well as in the sense determined there — have priority also over the third (just as over the second) motive of the moral action.

In this context, we shall not pursue the more psychological question as to which one of these three motives can factually be separated from the others.[81]

---

[81] It would probably show itself that the motivation of a moral action through morally relevant values which are not moral themselves or which are not understood as such can occur, in the case of the morally unconscious type, in isolation from the other two motives. On the other hand, neither being motivated by a moral value to be realized nor being motivated by the moral obligation can occur entirely isolated from an interest in one's own moral goodness. Being motivated by the moral obligation

Josef M. Seifert

(and by the moral value of one's own intervention) can, however, be isolated from being motivated by the morally relevant value, but only at the expense of a falsification of the moral act. We are concerned here not with purely empirical "psychological" questions, but with intelligible questions which are of great importance for ethics.

FOURTH RESPONSE:
THE UNIVERSALITY OF THE MOTIVE OF
THE MORAL ACTION

When we raise the question whether a moral agent can, in a concrete case, respond to all of the factors mentioned without being at the same time ready at least in principle to respond in a corresponding way also to similar factors of the same kind in other individual situations of acting, an only superficial glance at reality shows this to be impossible.

Since it is impossible, however, to will only one individual state of affairs characterized by morally relevant importance, to respect only one individual moral duty, to intend to realize only one individual moral value of an action, it shows itself that in the case of each morally good action, there is also a universal element co-motivating the action.[82]

In fact, we find that a different "universal object" corresponds to each of the three motivating factors discussed so far. All three motives of the moral action

---

[82]   See the literature mentioned in note 77.

discussed up to this point are, to be sure, entirely individual and unique: In a given situation, it is an entirely definite state of affairs which we are obligated to realize (we are, for example, not obligated to help suffering persons in general, but *one* suffering person); also, the concrete moral obligation is entirely individual, directing itself to us in a temporal and entirely personal way. Further, the moral value of each action also is in each case absolutely new and individual. It has a value in its own right which in its uniqueness cannot at all be dissolved into the value of a general attitude, virtue, or readiness in principle to act.[83] Each moral action adds a new value to the moral

---

[83]   In this context, it is to be noted that a virtue is much more than a mere readiness for action, and that it would also be a disastrous ethical mistake to dissolve the moral value of a virtue into the value of an action. That D. v. Hildebrand's ethics as well as that of Thomism acknowledge the value which a virtue has in itself as a *habitus* clearly overcomes the limitation of ethics to a doctrine about actions as we find it in Kant, for example. The case of a human who acts immorally in individual cases or areas in spite of a general will to act morally good illustrates two important states of affairs: On the one hand, it shows the fact that the general response to "all goods which impose obligations" which belongs to the essence of each morally good action is only *implicit,* or that it needs to be present only in the form of a basic intention. The moral response forming a part of each new moral action constitutes something entirely new over against this general good intention, even if he latter is fully "unfolded." On the other hand, this case also shows the conflict between the "general" response implied in each morally good action and a failure in a partial area of morality. Acting genuinely in a morally good way cannot possibly coexist without friction with other immoral actions. This is so only because of the fact that every good act has this intention towards generality.

world, irreplaceable by another action.

Simultaneously, however, and above each of these individual factors motivating the moral action, a different factor is present (albeit intimately linked with the individual factor) which also should motivate the moral action. An action would even cease to exist as a moral one if it would not at least implicitly be motivated also by the following three universal elements:

To begin with, the moral agent is motivated not only by the importance of the individual morally relevant state of affairs. Rather, he responds to much more than only to the individual morally relevant good; for all goods imposing obligations are also responded to at least implicitly. It is impossible to act in a morally good way while saying internally, as it were, "I will gladly do away with *this* want, with *this* misery; but in other similar situations in which I will be obligated to act, I will not do so." Raskolnikov in Dostoevsky's *Crime and Punishment* bows reverently not only before Sonja's suffering, but before the suffering of "all of humanity"; similarly, the person acting morally always responds implicitly to all goods imposing moral obligations.[84]

Also, the moral agent does not only affirm the

---

[84] Through this implicit response to all goods imposing obligations, an agent's moral goodness receives a character of transcending the individual situation; while the action as such remains limited to the individual case, the agent's "taking of an inner stand" goes beyond it.

individual moral demand which obligates him to his action, but implicitly at least he submits to all moral obligations wherever they may meet him; or he awakens within himself at least in principle a readiness to do this. This openness for the call, not only of this one moral obligation, but of all of them belongs so essentially to the substance of a moral action that such an action does not even come about if this readiness is lacking. One could call the "universal" factor behind the individual moral obligation "universal moral law" which is co-responded to — even if this expression is in some respects misleading.[85]

Finally, the interest in the individual moral value of a moral action goes hand in hand with an interest in the world of the morally good as a whole, an interest in all moral values in one's own person, but also in the moral goodness of other persons.[86] Inasmuch, however, as one should be interested in one's own moral goodness in an entirely different way since one is

---

[85] This is so because the expression "universal moral law," especially in its Kantian version, easily prevents an understanding of the way in which moral obligations are grounded in goods bearing values, as well as of the role the individual-concrete being has for ethics and for the concrete dimension of the moral obligation as addressing itself to the individual.

[86] This last aspect becomes clear as soon as one realizes how any interest in the moral which would be confined to moral values in one's own person would destroy itself; such an interest would end up in an egotism which would dissolve all morality. It belongs to the essence of the general will to be morally good that it also includes an interest in the realization of moral goodness in other persons.

immediately responsible only for one's own moral goodness, *this* universal motivating object of the moral action — that is, all moral goodness to be realized through ourselves — steps entirely into the foreground compared to the interest in the moral goodness of other persons as the general will that the morally good be done and moral evil ceases. One can designate the will directed at all the moral goodness to be realized through oneself which is a necessary foundation of all true moral actions also as the "general will to be morally good."[87] This general will to be morally good also is an indispensable component of moral consciousness, as well as of a true moral value of an action. Wherever this will is lacking, the moral value of the action would be deprived of its validity, and a merely accidental, morally unconscious character would inhere in the action.[88]

These three universal factors motivating a moral action must at least implicitly be present in each real moral action. Often, they assume even a fully conscious character and are probably experienced in some way by all moral agents. The consciousness of these universal motivating factors can often be noticed in everyday life

---

[87]   See the literature referred to in note 77.

[88]   With this, we have distinguished already three decisive elements which make the person who acts morally consciously different from the morally unconscious type: (1) The explicit response to the moral obligation (the moral call); (2) the explicit response to the moral value of one's own intervention; (3) the will pertaining to the three "general" motives of the moral action.

and in literature in expressions such as, "Never will I do such a mean thing," or, "I would tremble only if I could *ever* be unfaithful," (Constance in Mozart's opera *Abduction from the Seraglio*), or, "I will do what I have promised," and in similar examples; an analysis of language standing fully in the service of philosophic insight into the essence of things could examine very well the abundance of linguistic expressions in which the various universal motivating factors which have been mentioned as decisive for the moral action are formulated.

In the area of epistemology, nominalism as well as a "universalism" exaggerated along Averroistic lines — restricting our knowledge to universal species and genera — are mistaken.[89] Similarly, in the area of ethics, it is a fundamental mistake to exclude the role of universal motivating factors from morality, as well as intending to make them absolute. Situation ethics is clearly inclined towards the first fundamental mistake, Kant to the second. It is completely wrong to affirm that

---

[89] The thesis that our intellectual knowledge is confined to universals as it is found in Thomism stands in contrast to the Scotistic thesis that the intellect is also able to comprehend individuals as such, and that this ability co-determines decisively the special dignity of the intellect. Duns Scotus clearly sees the comprehension of the individual *as* individual as a decisive accomplishment of the intellect, and as the basis of all love for persons. See Josef Seifert, "Duns Scotus' Philosophie des Individuums und Kritik am Abstraktionismus der aristotelischen Erkenntnistheorie als grandioses Beispiel einer mit dem christlichen Glauben vereinbaren Philosophie," *Intus legere. Filosofía* Vol. 9, No. 2 (2015), pp. 111-124.

the moral agent would only respond to the individual factors of a moral situation, and neither apply universal moral principles, nor be motivated by them. It is, however, likewise a serious ethical mistake to overlook the full response to the concrete and individual situation, and to consider as the factors motivating the moral agent exclusively a "universal moral law," or "humanity as such" abstractly conceived, and similar factors.

As in so many other instances in philosophy, we are not concerned here with being in the middle of the road in overemphasizing neither the concrete situation and the individual motivating factors of the moral action, nor the universal factors. Rather, we are to emphasize the full uniqueness and the full weight of both. A clear comprehension and emphasis of the one does in no way lead one to overlooking the other. On the contrary, only a full acknowledgement of the recognition and response to the universal motivating factors allows one to see the true weight and the fateful, unique concreteness of a moral obligation, and vice versa. An ethics which, like situation ethics, does not wish to acknowledge universal principles and especially universal motivating factors of the moral action does not lead to a personalism which recognizes the dignity of the person and to a victory over an abstract ethical legalism. On the contrary, as we have seen above in our analysis of the moral obligation, the uniqueness of each moral situation and person reveals itself especially in the following: It is universally true that there is no good external to a person's action for the sake of which he may violate a moral duty. It would, however, be equally detrimental to — even destructive of — a full "turning towards" the individual situation (a situation in which marital fidelity is to be proved, for example) if the individual faithful action would not be accompanied by a general response to the value of fidelity, and potentially to *all* goods and obligations demanding faithfulness.[90]

---

[90] Once again, one could raise the question as to how this motive of the moral action would relate to the others. Only rarely will this motive be first in a *temporal* sense; strictly speaking, it can be temporally first only in the case of actions which are not morally obligatory, for example in the form of someone wishing to "do a good work" out of the general will to be morally good. In the case of morally obligatory actions, the general factors motivating the action appear in connection with and on the basis of the motivating factors discussed earlier. Further, these "general elements" do not motivate primarily the action's *will to realize*, but the antecedent response of the will to the morally relevant good in question.

FIFTH RESPONSE:
THE ABSOLUTE GOOD (GOD) AS MOTIVATING GROUND OF THE MORAL ACTION

As we continue to dwell on the nature of the moral action, a further reality motivating a moral action discloses itself. This motive can be lucidly conscious to the moral agent, but it can also be hidden, as it were, from the explicit consciousness of the moral agent. Upon deeper reflection, however, it becomes visible above all in the unconditional submission to the motive of the moral duty, the submission to the "breath of eternity," as Kierkegaard expresses himself. This obedience to the absolutely binding moral obligation contains, at least implicitly, also a submission to the absolute good, to God.

The deontological argument in support of God's existence attempts to discover through the objective essence of the moral "ought" the ground which makes its being possible.[91] To begin with, one can ask, "What is the ultimate ground of the obligation which factually addresses itself to us, what is, as it were, the ultimate *causa efficiens* of the moral duty which can be immediately experienced and which is connected with the morally relevant realities?"[92] It would become manifest (as cannot be explained in more detail here) that the moral obligation would, in its majesty and absoluteness as a personal "call" — a call which is most of the time much more absolute than the goods from which it proceeds — remain metaphysically unexplained and be deprived of its ultimate ground of being if it would not be rooted in the absolute divine personal being who addresses me personally in and through the moral obligation. This is revealed even more clearly through the moment of personally being called to account which discloses itself, especially in the

---

[91]   I have developed this argument broadly in Josef Seifert, *Erkenntnis des Vollkommenen. Wege der Vernunft zu Gott* (Bonn: Lepanto Verlag, 2010), Chapter 5, pp. 81-108; the same author, *Conocimiento de Dios por las vías de la razón y del amor.* Traducido por Pedro Jesús Teruel, revisado y aumentado por el autor (Madrid: Encuentro, 2013), Chapter 5, pp. 87-118.

[92]   We can speak here of *causa efficiens* only inasmuch as the concept of an efficient cause is compatible with the intelligible "groundedness" of the moral obligation in the state of affairs to be realized, and in the importance of this state of affairs. A moral obligation cannot be called into existence like a thing through a *causa efficiens.* Again, it is rooted in the special uniqueness of the moral obligation that an entirely special efficient cause corresponds to it (in the sense of a person "speaking through it," grounding its ultimate metaphysically binding force).

voice of conscience, through the "being responsible" accompanying the moral obligation.[93] Even a specifically ethical investigation of the moral agent's response to a moral obligation shows clearly, however, that he responds, whether or not he knows it, in the moral action at least implicitly to God and, unlike in any other situation, affirms or rejects him. The unconditional character of the submission which is demanded by the moral obligation, its seriousness, includes — in contrast to a response to a work of art as such — necessarily an (implicit) response to God as the one who reveals himself through the very nature of the moral obligation as the Lord over our life. This is the reason why the fate of someone who does not know God through no fault of his own is determined on the basis of his moral decisions in which God is either accepted or rejected.[94] Even the noble "pagan" often

---

[93] See on this point above all J. H. Newman, *Grammar of Assent*, Chapter 5, section 1, pp. 97 ff. This "being responsible" is founded on the one hand on the freedom of the person, on the other on the unique weight of the moral obligation as well as of the reality grounding it. R. Ingarden has thoughtfully examined the essence of responsibility and its ontological presuppositions. In this context, Ingarden shows in particular how the objectivity of values, the identity of the subject, the structure of the person as substance, his freedom, and the causal and temporal structure of the world are, in different ways, ontological presuppositions of responsibility. See R. Ingarden, *Über die Verantwortung*, pp. 35 ff.

[94] This relationship of morality to God which has often been recognized already in antiquity (see note 95) finds, in the light of faith, its explicit confirmation in the passages of Paul regarding the pagans, who are judged according to the testimony of their conscience (Rom 2.14-16). D. v. Hildebrand has pertinently

consciously recognizes this, such as Socrates:

> *Men of Athens, I am devoted to you, and I*
> *love you; but I shall be obedient to the God*
> *more than to you, and as long as I am*
> *breathing and able to, I will not cease to look*
> *for wisdom, and to exhort you.*[95]

The essential nature of this motive for the realization of the moral value of an action becomes especially clear whenever it is explicitly rejected,[96] in an attitude of *ressentiment*, for example.[97] As M. Scheler has shown, a moral action loses its moral value entirely if it closes itself to this ultimate motivating ground and object, and explicitly declines it full of resentment.[98] Kant's express rejection of this motivating ground amounts to a philosophical destruction of the substance

---

analyzed the basis of this relationship. See D. v. Hildebrand, *The Nature of Love*, pp. 85 ff.

[95]   Plato, *Apology*, 29D.

[96]   D. v. Hildebrand has shown this clearly in *Die Menschheit am Scheideweg*, pp. 56 ff.

[97]   M. Scheler has analyzed this attitude of resentment in detail in his monograph, *Das Ressentiment im Aufbau der Moralen*. The book has been translated by William W Holdheim and published, as *Ressentiment*, in 1961, with an Introduction by Lewis A. Coser (New York: Free Press of Glencoe 1961); reprint: New York: Schocken Books, 1972. Second edition: Introduction by Manfred S. Frings, (Milwaukee: Marquette University Press, 1994).

[98]   See M. Scheler, *Das Ressentiment im Aufbau der Moralen*, pp. 96-107.

of the moral act.[99] This becomes especially clear when we think also of the fact that the validity of the motivation of the moral action by its own moral value remains preserved only as long as this value is intended, implicitly at least, in its transcendent openness to God. If the moral value is, as is done in Kant's principle of autonomy, explicitly made absolute in the sense of being expressly alienated from its ultimate calling as a glorification of God, the living embodiment of all moral goodness and of all values, an application of this principle to the moral life would lead to a destruction of the moral value of an action, and to a perversion of the moral act; even more, an action which is in this way explicitly cut off from the motive of a response to God is a bearer of a moral disvalue; ultimately, even of a diabolical moral disvalue of rebellion against God, of an attempt to make oneself into God.[100]

This fifth motive of the moral action is in itself especially compatible with being merely implicit, with not becoming conscious in an individual moral action: Even a moral act in which this motive is not at all actually present, but which is "open" to it, is a bearer of a genuine moral value.[101]

---

[99]   See I. Kant, *Groundwork*, pp. 111-112, *Practical Reason*, p. 241 ff., *Metaphysics of Morals*, A 109.

[100]   See notes 98 and 99.

[101]   As long as one understands the concept of the "anonymous Christian" as K. Rahner has introduced it exclusively in this sense, this concept can find its legitimate interpretation. As soon,

In some respects, this motive (or rather the openness for it) is so profoundly and essentially connected with all other motives of the moral action and constitutes within itself the relation to the highest value of creation, the glorification of God, that it must be designated as the most important and deepest motive of all acting morally. This is expressed also on the religious level when within supernatural morality, the love of God constitutes the ultimate ground and the final motive of all moral acting.[102] At the same time, however, this motive of the moral action is organically built upon the others. Frequently, it motivates the moral action "through" the other elements, and it can be understood correctly as a motive of the morally obligatory action of the atheist only when all other motivating factors of the moral action also are clearly comprehended.[103] Indeed, in such a case it constitutes, because of its being grounded and "dependent" on the other motives of the moral action, their "ultimate" motive. For the special acceptance or rejection of God in

---

however, as one overlooks the entirely new value of the actions motivated explicitly and consciously by God (the glorification of God), or as soon as one understands this new value (and especially the transition to the Christian faith) only like a transition from the "implicit" to the "explicit," we are confronted with a grave philosophical and theological error which overlooks what radical influence the *explicit* knowledge of truth and the conscious being motivated by it has on the moral value of an act.

[102] See note 25.

[103] Without this, the moment of the moral obligation in general would be unintelligible, and with it, the morally *obligatory* action.

the moral and immoral action by *its very nature*, even when performed by the atheist, can be understood and exists only after a recognition of the other motivating factors of the moral action.

A more thorough examination of the relation between the morally good action and an affirmation of God cannot be presented here.[104]

---

[104] See J. Seifert, *Erkenntnis des Vollkommenen*, Chapter 5; *Conocimiento de Dios por las vías de la razón y del amor*, Chapter 5.

SIXTH RESPONSE: THE MOTIVATING ROLE OF ONE'S OWN HAPPINESS FOR THE MORAL ACTION

When we consider only the motives of the moral action dealt with so far, the moral act seems to be exclusively and purely a surrender, an act characterized by a unique transcendence. Thus, it shows itself to be motivated by the importance of the morally relevant object, by the obedience to the moral duty, by the value-responding interest in the moral value of the action, and finally, by an acceptance or rejection of the absolute good.

And indeed, we find all of these dimensions of surrender and transcendence as sources of the unique value of the moral action. Any eudemonism or even more any hedonism, locking humans in the moral act into an immanent striving for happiness where one's own happiness is the ultimate and only motive of moral acts, constitute a fundamental error and a falsification of the moral. And although this error stands, as mentioned already, in a blatant contradiction to the theological view of medieval philosophers/theologians, they have time and again maintained it in different forms. Fénelon rightly protests against this error of immanentism in ethics which Bossuet, for example, maintains.[105] But his reaction constitutes a typically false one.[106] It is also a grave ethical error to maintain that it must belong to the essence of the moral act to be disinterested in one's own

---

[105] See the analysis of these positions in R. Spaemann's book, *Spontaneität und Reflexion*, pp. 26 ff., pp. 81 ff.

[106] I cannot pursue attempts intending to dissolve, to a certain extent, the contrasts of opinion between Fénelon and Bossuet. For a critique of this view of Fénelon, see D. v. Hildebrand, *The Nature of Love*, pp. 139 ff., pp. 205 ff.; simultaneously, the same book radically overcomes moral eudemonism. See also my book, *True Love* (South Bend, Indiana: St. Augustine Press, 2015), especially pp. 43-51; R. Spaemann, *op. cit.*, pp. 81 ff., 108 ff., as well as Josef Seifert, "Karol Cardinal Wojtyła (Pope John Paul II)   as Philosopher and the Cracow/Lublin School of Philosophy" in *Aletheia* II (1981), pp. 130-199; the same author, "Verdad, Libertad y Amor en el Pensiamento Antropologico y Etico de Karol Wojtyła," in *Persona y Derecho*, Navarra (1983), pp. 177-193. Also published in *Veritas II* (Monterrey, N.L., Mexico: Universidad Regiomontana, 1983); "A volontade como perfeição pura e a nova concepção não-eudemonística do amor segundo Duns Scotus," traduzido do inglés por Roberto Hofmeister Pich, *Veritas* (Philosophische Fakultät, PUCRS, Porto Alegre, Brasilien: September 2005), pp. 51-84.
    It seems clear that, when Fénelon speaks of amour désintéressé, he has in mind a love which is entirely independent at least of all motivation by one's own happiness, but which remains also in a certain indifference to one's own happiness. See the passages from Fénelon which Spaemann quotes in *op. cit.*, p 77 (note 42); p. 76 (note 39); p. 73 (note 29 and 30); see above all p. 49 and the passages referred to there.

happiness, to consider this act as an "amour pur" which supposedly is incompatible with any being motivated by one's own happiness, even with an interest in one's own happiness which is essentially connected with the moral act. One must avoid this mistake to be found on both sides of the famous ethical debate (between Fénelon and his opponents), and to overcome it truly, as has been done in our century, without having found yet the deserved recognition on the part of philosophers of ethics.[107]

The "amour désintéressé" is not only "de facto impracticable, as if there would have to be in humans some kind of coexistence between morality and egoism," as has been suggested time and again since Plato's *Philebus*.[108]

Rather, the thought of an amour désintéressé, which leads to an existential nihilism, falsifies the necessary connection between the moral surrender and one's own final, ultimate good; thus, it falsifies the essence of the moral surrender itself.

The moral agent does and also ought to strive essentially for that peace, that happiness, and that participation in the good which the moral act affords. It constitutes a serious error on the part of Fénelon and in

---

[107] Beginnings for this can be found in M. Scheler; a final systematic refutation of eudemonism and simultaneously of the position of a Stoical indifferentism to one's own happiness à la Fénelon can be found in D. v. Hildebrand. See note 106.

[108] See Plato, *Philebus*, 13 c ff., 20 b ff.

our time on the part of Hartshorne, for example,[109] to see in this striving an egotistical element which falsifies morality. This striving for participation in the good and for the happiness of being united with it can be found, albeit in a different form, also in the *intentio unionis* characterizing all of love, an *intentio* which D. v. Hildebrand has thoroughly investigated in his work *The Nature of Love*.[110]

The question arises, however, whether and how this striving for happiness can occur as a motive of love or of a moral action, or whether it is connected with the moral action only in a different, albeit necessary way: that of a non-intended "superabundant" consequence of the morally good action.

A first response to this question could be that striving for happiness cannot constitute a motive of the moral action. One could acknowledge, to be sure, with Max Scheler, for example, a necessary connection between acting morally and happiness, but only such that happiness is either a necessary presupposition of moral goodness or a necessary consequence of the moral action.[111] One could rightly and profoundly point

---

[109] In his writings on process theology, Hartshorne represents most radically the viewpoint of a morality which is uninterested in happiness. Each thinking about personal immortality, reward, or aiming for happiness seems to be for him a defilement of morality. This is one of the reasons for the strong opposition on the part of Hartshorne against all traditional Christianity with its promise of eternal beatitude.

[110] *The Nature of Love*, pp. 123 ff.; see also pp. 109 ff.

[111] See M. Scheler, *Formalism*, pp. 328 ff. M. Scheler

out that happiness need in no way appear as a conscious motive of the moral action, or that it does perhaps not at all appear as such. Above all, one could entirely correctly put forward the fact that for the reasons explained earlier, happiness can obviously not be the primary motive of moral actions. And on this basis, one could point out a threefold necessary connection of happiness and the moral action and of happiness as the consequence of the latter: One could point out first how a kind of inner happiness and peace is a state inseparably connected with acting in a morally good way. Entirely rightly, one could call, in this context, attention to the fact that this happiness appears superabundantly[112] precisely because the moral agent

---

acknowledges these two kinds of necessary connections between happiness and morality, and sees a false alternative in opposing them. See *ibid.*, p. 359: "All feelings of happiness and unhappiness have their foundation in feelings of values. Deepest happiness and complete bliss are dependent in their being on a consciousness of one's own moral goodness. Only the good person is blissful. This does not preclude the possibility that this very blissfulness is the root and source of all willing and acting. But happiness can never be a goal or even a 'purpose' of willing and acting. Only the happy person acts in a morally good way. Happiness is therefore in no way a 'reward for virtue,' nor is virtue a means to reach blissfulness. Nevertheless, happiness is the root and source of virtue, a fountainhead, although it is only a consequence of the inner goodness of the person."

[112] By "superabundance" or "superabundant relation," we mean a relation in which one reality has another meaningfully as a consequence, and even serves this other reality, without, however, being a mere means. In many cases, the "first" reality within a superabundant relation is to be taken seriously not only in itself (i.e. not as a mere means), but it is even more important than the

"forgets himself" in a certain way and transcends himself in being directed entirely to the state of affairs to be realized, to the fulfillment of the obligation, and so on. His happiness accrues to him precisely because it is not the primary motive for his turning towards the object; happiness is exactly tied inseparably to the prerequisite of the transcendence of the moral response.[113] Further, one could point out that the person who acts in a morally good way is objectively worthy of happiness, or deserves happiness in the form of a reward.[114] Here, one refers to another happiness, bestowed from the outside and by a moral authority, a happiness differing from the inner happiness connected with the moral action.[115] Moreover, one could rightly point out that this happiness also should be bestowed onto the agent precisely because it did not constitute the motive of his action. One could finally point out: Even if one prescinds from the reward and even if one does not

---

second reality which is its consequence. In the case of morality, for example, the value proper to morality is clearly superior to that of happiness, the superabundant consequence of the former.

[113] See D. v. Hildebrand, *Ethics*, pp. 36 ff., and *The Nature of Love*, pp. 101 ff.

[114] Kant has emphasized this relationship. Scheler rejects it. This relationship, which cannot be investigated more closely here, obtains without question, even if in its Kantian conception, it is falsified and often altogether misinterpreted. In his *Die Menschheit am Scheideweg*, pp. 517 ff., D. v. Hildebrand elaborates, as a part of a theological-religious essay, the essence of the relationship between moral goodness and reward.

[115] *Ibid.*, pp. 518 ff.

consider the extreme case of a moral agent tortured externally, it can be determined that in the normal circumstances of life, preserved free from extreme and eternal suffering, a deep happiness (of a martyr, for example, or of the imprisoned Florestan in Beethoven's opera *Fidelio*) accrues superabundantly to the person acting morally, a happiness radiating from the inner harmony of his conscience into his entire life. This happiness can be enhanced in manifold ways by many consequences of his moral goodness, in his friendships, in his love to his wife or to his children, and so on.

One will say that all these dimensions of the happiness connected with the moral action stand not only in an accidental, but more or less in a necessary relation to the moral action. In all of them, however, happiness surely is always only a consequence, never a motive of the moral action.

Without intending to deny the truth of this answer which in fact does justice to many aspects of the relationship between happiness and morality, still a second answer to our question must be given. Let us assume someone were to ask us, "Do you want to become happy, do you aim at becoming happy?" Let us further suppose that we would respond, "No, we strive only for objective goals; only these motivate us, but not our happiness." It becomes quickly apparent that this answer is artificial. And if we also would add, "We are motivated only by moral goodness; there is no striving present in us which explicitly asks for our own happiness," such an answer shows itself not only as unnatural, but also as immoral, for we neglect in it the moral relevance of happiness and persist in a prideful self-sufficiency. For we are strictly morally obligated to strive for our own happiness, and this obligation does not mean that we ought to strive for any form of pleasure or happiness on the basis of a natural instinct in us, as we do anyway; rather, this moral duty means that we ought to strive for our *true*, deepest happiness, for that which makes us permanently and profoundly happy. And this striving is not necessarily present in us, as is demonstrated through the case of the person who carelessly risks his life, the superficial person, the immoral person, the person committing suicide, or the person who is even completely oblivious to his eternal blessedness or the threat of his eternal damnation. We are morally obligated to true self-love, to be interested in this our *true* happiness, to do everything leading to it, to avoid everything leading away from it. This striving for our true happiness is not an inevitable trait of human nature but an important and rare moral virtue.[116] Happiness plays now doubtlessly a motivating role for this morally obligatory striving.

One could object, however, that this happiness indeed motivates, as its immediate objects, a striving and a hope, but that it does not motivate the moral *action*.

A complex answer to this very difficult ethical problem seems correct to us: Our happiness is surely

---

[116] Thomas Aquinas emphasizes that not all humans strive for this *true* happiness. See *Summa Theologica*, I-II, q. 51.-8.

not the *primary* motive of the moral action, and inasmuch as happiness necessarily follows the moral action, it is the latter's superabundant consequence — be it as inner peace or as a reward. The primary motivating factors of the moral action have been shown already.

On the other hand, a desire to participate in the inner harmony and in the happiness flowing from what is morally good grows necessarily out of the agent's will directed to what is morally good. The moral agent is filled with the desire for a union with the good, with the goods constituting the origin of the moral ought, and above all with the absolute good to which each moral action is ultimately directed, as we have seen. This longing for participation in the good is similar to the longing for a union with the beloved which is characteristic of each love. Just as this longing for union is necessarily connected with love, so is the longing for participation in the good necessarily connected with the moral action. And just as the longing for union with the beloved does not have a selfish character, but occurs primarily "out of love" and for the sake of the beloved so that he can be loved more based on an always growing cognition of his person and through the unity with him, so does the longing for the participation in the good, above all in the absolute good, aim chiefly and most deeply at reaching through it, in full purity and contemplative peace, the moral self-surrender which is threatened by many obstacles and subject to many disturbances. But, just as in love the longing for union with the beloved is also filled with the theme of the happiness growing out of this union, so also is the theme of becoming happy oneself fully present in the longing for participation in and union with the "good," the "absolute good," a longing which goes hand in hand with the moral action (and indeed with all of morality). And not only is this theme not opposed to the surrender to the moral obligation and the goods in which this obligation is grounded; rather, it is morally obligatory to strive *also* for this ultimate happiness, *not* to be indifferent to it, to long for it. This striving for happiness does not in the least constitute a change of the inner direction of the surrender to the good and a turning back onto oneself; rather, because of its superabundant character, it is a feature of this happiness that the pure striving for it grows precisely out of the depth of this surrender, that it constitutes an augmentation of this surrender, so that we may say, comparing love and morality: A person longs so deeply for the happiness growing out of the surrender of love and of the presence of the beloved because he loves the beloved so deeply for his own sake; similarly, the moral agent strives ultimately also for a participation in what is good in itself and for the happiness growing out of the surrender to it because he wants the morally good for its own sake, but *in no way* as a means for his happiness.[117]

---

[117] In *The Nature of Love*, pp. 118 ff., D. v. Hildebrand shows impressively how the longing for the happiness of the union with the beloved does not in the least detract from the surrender to him

In contrast to love, the striving for happiness connected with the moral action is also linked with the awareness that happiness is and should be a reward for goodness.[118]

The happiness of love is, on the other hand, a theme in an entirely different sense, inasmuch as above all, the being of the beloved and the union with him are consciously experienced and desired as a source of happiness. Nevertheless, even if we prescind here from the case of caritas (*agape*) in which morality and love "coincide" most fully, happiness still is in a threefold respect more deeply thematic in the moral action than in any type of human love. First, our *ultimate* happiness and our deepest inner peace are doubtlessly connected with acting morally, but not with human love as such. Second, happiness stands in a more necessary and more metaphysical relationship to acting morally than to human love. While the latter may be "disappointed" and therefore "unhappy," happiness, specifically in the form of "ultimate happiness," is much more essentially connected with the morally good action — even in the case of the most tragic external circumstances. There is no tragic or unhappy moral goodness, whereas there

---

for his own sake, or opposes to the transcendent "direction" an egotistical one; he shows that on the contrary, this striving for happiness and unity increases the surrender and that love can, therefore, be called a "super-value-response."

[118] It shall not be discussed in detail how happiness is not only the reward of goodness, but can, *as such*, also co-motivate moral actions. See the works quoted in notes 111 and 113-115.

are many cases of tragic and unhappy love. Third, in the moral action, happiness is not only experienced and aimed at, but through this action, it is also "deserved" as a reward; because of this, happiness stands in a much deeper metaphysical relationship to the moral action than it does to human love if the latter is not transformed by charity in which case it coincides with the most profound dimension of moral goodness.[119]

The question remains, however, whether this striving for happiness connected with the moral action also means that happiness motivates the moral agent, and specifically the moral action itself. Indeed, the question arises as to whether a superabundant consequence of an act can simultaneously be the motive of this act.

This seems quite possible, provided one distinguishes between the primary motives of an act chiefly bringing it about and subordinate (secondary) motives. The latter ones are reasons for acting which motivate, in a subordinate way, both a striving (in our case a striving for happiness) which is necessarily connected with an act as well as the act (the moral action itself). This does not constitute an opposition to the surrender characterizing the moral action; rather, it grows out of this surrender when the agent speaks, as it were, "I am fulfilling this moral obligation simply because the good to be realized demands this effort, because I owe absolute subordination to the moral

---

[119] See on this, D. von Hildebrand, *The Nature of Love*, Chapter 11.

obligation, because I want to be morally good, and finally, because I wish through my action to respond to God's call to me, to glorify him. These are the first and primary motives for my acting — already sufficient in themselves. But in acting for these reasons, I am striving also for participation in the good, in its inner harmony, for the happiness growing from it: Most of all, to complete the surrender to the good, but also for the sake of the ultimate and irreplaceable gift of my inner peace and of the happiness which will grow from the good, and for which I am even obligated to strive. I act well also because I am aware that doing so is a condition for my ultimate and unrenounceable happiness, and that my being destined for this happiness demands that I act in this way. This happiness motivates me in my acting in a subordinate, but unrenounceable[120] way, but as something growing

---

[120] The readiness to forego one's own happiness because of a superordinate point of view is, of course, in many cases noble and even morally obligatory. We should not even hold on to our "ultimate happiness" such that we *would* not be ready to forego it if this would be obligatory for reasons of what is good in itself. The unrenounceability of one's own happiness is to mean only the following: *First*, we are obligated also to strive for our own happiness; therefore, we may not forego it without reason. *Second*, it would diminish our surrender to what is good in itself if we were to forego our own happiness; for the well-ordered longing for happiness in the sense of the "super-value-response" deepens one's own surrender, and is, for this reason, "unrenounceable." *Third*, there is, as a consequence of what has just been stated, an "ultimate point" of a longing for one's own happiness which is inseparable from the surrender connected with the good in a way such that foregoing it "absolutely" would be "nihilistic," and

precisely out of forgetting oneself when doing what is good."

This final motive of the moral action is, according to its essence, entirely subordinated to the others. Making happiness into the goal of acting morally and the latter into a means for this goal constitutes the basic mistake of eudemonism.

The basic mistake of Fénelon and others is, however, to overlook that happiness *is* aimed for at the place appropriate to it, and that it *ought* to be aimed at, that we ultimately ought to be concerned with it, and that it ought to motivate our moral acting in a subordinate way without this clouding the purity of the moral surrender.

---

incompatible with the necessary essence of the relationship between morality and happiness.

CONCLUSION

It goes hand in hand with the elements mentioned as motivating the moral action that acting is, on the one hand, *eo ipso* active, but that on the other hand, it simultaneously aims at a union with the absolute and eternal good in contemplative acts. As Aristotle outstandingly emphasizes, the contemplative life is superior to the active life and leads the latter essentially to the former; or rather, in acting, humans aim essentially at a contemplative life.[121] This can also be

---

[121] Aristotle, *Nicomachean Ethics*, X, VII, 5 ff. The superiority of the contemplative life over the practical which Aristotle demonstrates masterfully in this work must sharply be distinguished from his false thesis that the dianoetic virtues, or the intellect and its fulfillment, are higher than the moral virtues. This error stems from a limitation of the contemplative life to the sphere of the intellect rather than seeing the eminently contemplative character of moral acts, as especially of love, and simultaneously, from overlooking the fact that the degree of "contemplativeness" of an act is only *one* value criterion among others, and that the moral values possess, because of their groundedness in freedom, and because they alone, not knowledge per se, make the person qua person morally good, a unique

found in the moral action. The moral agent aims ultimately at the surrender to and the union with something eternal which breaks into his life in the moral obligation and in the moral striving, and at the union with this eternal; and thus, all moral acting is inseparably connected with a being directed at immortality. This relationship between morality and immortality cannot be considered any further here.[122]

We cannot discuss here other motives which in the beginning were designated as "subjective," and which depend on the particular ethical being of the individual moral agent. How acting morally can be motivated by dispositions and virtues of a person, such as by love and by what the great thinkers of the middle

---

primacy over all other values.

[122] Cf. on this relationship Josef Seifert: "¿Tenemos y somos un alma espiritual e inmortal?" in Carlos Casanova (ed.), Josef Seifert, and Daniel von Wachter, *El alma, la providencia y el derecho natural (un ejercicio de filosofía como capacidad de juzgar):* conferencia de cierre de la International Academy of Philosophy at the Pontificia Universidad Católica de CHILE (2015), pp. 11-40; "Das Unsterblichkeitsproblem aus der Sicht der philosophischen Ethik und Anthropologie," *Franziskanische Studien,* H 3 (1978); Filosofie, Pravda, Nesmrtlenost. Tòi praúskå pòednáóky/Philosophie, Wahrheit, Unsterblichkeit. Drei Prager Vorlesungen/ Philosophy, Truth, Immortality. Three Prague Lectures (tschechisch-deutsch), pòeklad, úvod a bibliografi Martin Cajthaml (Prague: Vydala Kòestanská akademie Òim, svacek, edice Studium, 1998); "Philosophizing with Plato about the Immortality of the Soul," *Philosophical News.* No. 8 marzo 2014, *Anima,* pp. 140-162; "¿Poseemos y somos un alma inmortal?" *Philosophia,* 73, 1 (2013), pp. 13-42.

ages have called the *bonum diffusivum sui*[123] is a central topic of ethics, as well as how these motives are above all the most profound grounds for acting which is morally good but not morally obligatory. Although this essay is limited to a study of morally obligatory actions, we do not at all intend to question the depth of these topics and their quality of reaching into the deepest grounds of morality.

If someone thinks that the understanding of the motivation of the moral action presented here is too complex and would have to give way to Ockham's principle prohibiting a multiplication of principles, if someone thinks it to be contrary to the essence of philosophy as directed towards unity to acknowledge so many motivating factors of the moral action, we can only respond with Ross that the question of whether one principle or many are to be used to explain a being is to be decided only on the basis of reality.[124] In all cases in which a general essence or a unity exists, it is certainly a task of philosophy to discover it rather than incorrectly and unnecessarily multiplying principles or remaining at a multiplicity which could be reduced to a unity. Whenever, though, a unity in the form of identity is not present, a reduction to unity is a monism or a reductionism which is contrary to true philosophy.

---

[123] The great medieval philosophers and with them the Catholic Church recognize this inner diffusiveness, this "outward-flowing," this self-communication of the good as (a) main motive of God's creation of the world.

[124] See Note 63.

There is nothing which speaks *a priori* in favor of a reduction to unity, let alone to identity, in all parts and all respects of reality as being more appropriate than an acknowledgement of various elements and realities. A recognition of the difference between mind and matter or between God and the world is in no way *a priori* philosophically inferior to monism or pantheism. On the contrary, an investigation conforming to reality shows these reductions of reality to "one principle" as mistaken, and at the same time, to be a blocking off of the road leading to a recognition of the true inner *unity* of reality, a unity which is in no way contrary to the diversity, the differentiation of being, but even requires it.[125]

Moreover, if the view of the motivation of the moral action presented here is viewed as too "idealistic" because it supposedly presupposes a "pure" motivation of the moral action which does not take into account the motivation of humans in which surrender and egoism factually are mixed, we respond that our analysis is entirely compatible with the realism contained in Solzhenitsyn's words:

> "*The line separating good and evil does not run between classes and parties, but straight through the heart of every human being. This line is moveable; it vacillates over the course of the years. Even in a heart occupied by evil, a bridgehead of goodness maintains itself. Even*

---

[125]   See J. Seifert, *Leib und Seele*, especially pp. 170 ff.; 83 ff.

in the best heart, there remains an unconquerable hiding place of evil. (Motto for Gulag Archipelago II.)

This statement holds certainly true for all of us. An ethical analysis of the moral action and of its motivation does, however, not have the task to conform to empirical-sociological facts or to reproduce them. Rather, the ethical analysis has a function which is self-critical and critical of society in the best sense of this word: Beginning with an experience of the essence[126] of what the morally good action is "itself" and of its motivation which makes, to the extent to which it is realized, an action into a morally good one, we may gaze into the timeless mirror in which we are able to recognize whether and to what extent the motivation of *our actions* makes them into moral ones.[127]

---

[126] See on this J. Seifert, *Erkenntnis objektiver Wahrheit*, pp. 151 ff., 266 ff. See especially B. Schwarz, "D. v. Hildebrand's Lehre von der 'Soseinserfahrung' in ihren philosophiegeschichtlichen Zusammenhängen," in *Wahrheit, Wert und Sein*, pp. 33 ff.

[127] The famous Austrian writer of comedies Johann Nestroy has expressed this in an extremely witty comparison, (based on the double meaning of the German word "Handlung" that can mean both action and store that cannot be translated into English), between splendid luxury stores (*Handlungen*) in Vienna and human actions (*Handlungen*), which are very rarely beautiful, noble, and chivalry-like such that quite few of them could bear the radiant light which illuminates those splendid human stores. See Johann Nestroy, "Einen Jux will er sich machen, " I, 10, iii. See also Josef Seifert, *Heitere Philosophie – Philosophieren mit Johann Nestroy, dem witzigsten österreichischen Philosophen* (Mainz: Patrimonium-Verlag, 2016).

BIBLIOGRAPHY

Anselm of Canterbury. *Opera Omnia.* F. S. Schmitt, ed. Stuttgart-Bad Cannstatt, 1968.

———. *De Veritate.* In *Opera Omnia.* Vol. 1. pp. 169 ff.

———. *Werke (Leben, Lehre, Werke des hl. Anselm von Canterbury).* R. Allers, ed. Vienna, 1963.

Aristotle. *Nicomachean Ethics.* London, 1962.

Augustinus, Aurelius. *Confessionum Libri XIII.* Heinrich Wangnereck, ed. Turin, 1962.

Bonaventura. *Opera Omnia.* Quaracchi, 1882-1902.

Brentano, Franz. *Vom Ursprung sittlicher Erkenntnis.* 5th ed. Hamburg, 1965.

Copleston, Frederick. *A History of Philosophy.* Vol. 8 (Part II). New York, 1967.

Fletcher, Joseph. *Situation Ethics.* Philadelphia, 1966.

Hengstenberg, Hans-Eduard. *Grundlegung der Ethik.* Stuttgart, 1969.

Hildebrand, Dietrich von: *Die Idee der sittlichen Handlung and Sittlichkeit und ethische Werterkenntnis.* 2nd ed. Darmstadt, 1969.

———. *Die Menschheit am Scheideweg.* Regensburg, 1955.

———, ed. *Rehabilitierung der Philosophie. Festgabe für Balduin Schwarz zum 70. Geburtstag.* Stuttgart, 1974.

———. *Ethics.* Chicago, 1972.

———. *Moralia.* Vol. 9 of *Gesammelte Werke.* Stuttgart, 1980.

———. *The Nature of Love.* John F. Crosby and John Henry Crosby, trans. South Bend, 2009.

————. *What is Philosophy?* With an introductory essay by Josef Seifert. 3d ed. London, 1991.

———— and Alice von Hildebrand. *Morality and Situation Ethics*. 2nd ed. Chicago, 1966.

Hildebrand, Alice von. "Near-sightedness of Keen Thinkers — A Critical Study of G. E. Moore." In *Rehabilitierung der Philosophie*. Dietrich von Hildebrand, ed. Regensburg, 1974. pp. 157-173.

————. "On the Pseudo-obvious." In *Wahrheit, Wert und Sein. Festgabe für Dietrich von Hildebrand zum 80. Geburtstag*. Balduin Schwarz, ed. Stuttgart, 1970. pp 25-32.

Ingarden, Roman. *Über die Verantwortung. Ihre ontologischen Fundamente*. Stuttgart, 1970.

Kant, Immanuel. *Critique of Practical Reason and Other Writings on Moral Philosophy*. Lewis White Beck, trans. Chicago, 1949.

————. *Groundwork of the Metaphysic of Morals*. H. J. Paton, trans. New York, 1964.

Kierkegaard, Soren. *Concluding unscientific Postscripts to Philosophical Fragments*. Vol. 1. Howard V. Hong and Edna H. Hong, trans. and ed. Princeton, 1992.

Laun, Andreas. *Die naturrechtliche Begründung der Ethik in der Neueren Katholischen Moraltheologie*. Wien, 1973.

Mill, John Stuart. *Utilitarianism*. 2nd edition. 1884.

Moore, Georg Eduard. *Principia Ethica*. 14th ed. London, 1971.

Nestroy, Johann. "Einen Jux will er sich machen." In *Gesammelte Werke*, Vol. 3. Wien, 1962.

Newman, John Henry. *Grammar of Assent.* 2nd edition. New York, 1958.

Pfänder, Alexander. *Phänomenologie des Wollens. Motive und Motivation.* München, 1963.

Plato. *Gorgias; Apology; Philebus.* In *Sämtliche Werke.* Vol. 1 and 5. Hamburg, 1959-1964.

Fromm, Matthias. *Katholische Glaubenskunde. Ein Lehrbuch der Dogmatik.* 4 volumes. Vol. 1. 3d ed. Wien, 1961.

Reinach, Adolf. "The A priori Foundations of the Civil Law." John F. Crosby, trans. In *Aletheia — An International Journal of Philosophy,* Vol. 3. (1983), pp. 28 ff.

Reiner, Hans. *Die philosophische Ethik.* Heidelberg, 1964.

———. *Pflicht und Neigung.* Meisenheim/Glan, 1951.

Ross, Sir W. David. *Foundations of Ethics.* 4th ed. 1960.

Scheler, Max. *Der Formalismus in der Ethik und die materiale Wertethik.* 5th ed. *Gesammelte Werke,* Vol. 2. Bern-München, 1966.

———. *Das Ressentiment im Aufbau der Moralen.* In *Vom Umsturz der Werte. Gesammelte Werke,* Vol. 3. Bern-München, 1955. English editions: *Ressentiment.* William W. Holdheim, trans. First edition, edited with an Introduction by Lewis A. Coser. New York: Free Press of Glencoe, 1961. Reprint: New York: Schocken Books, 1972. Second edition with an Introduction by Manfred S. Frings. Milwaukee, 1994.

Schwarz, Balduin. "D. v. Hildebrand's Lehre von der 'Soseinserfahrung' in ihren philosophiegeschichtlichen Zusammenhängen." In *Wahrheit, Wert und Sein*. Balduin Schwarz, ed. pp. 33 ff.

————, ed. *Wahrheit, Wert und Sein. Festgabe für Dietrich von Hildebrand zum 80. Geburtstag*. Stuttgart, 1970.

Seifert, Josef. "A volontade como perfeição pura e a nova concepção não-eudemonística do amor segundo Duns Scotus." Roberto Hofmeister Pich, trans. *Veritas*. Philosophische Fakultät, PUCRS, Porto Alegre, Brazil, September 2005.

————. "Absolute Moral Obligations towards Finite Goods as Foundation of Intrinsically Right and Wrong Actions. A Critique of Consequentialist Teleological Ethics: Destruction of Ethics through Moral Theology?" *Anthropos* 1 (1985): 57-94.

————. *Back to Things in Themselves. A phenomenological Foundation for Classical Realism*. 2nd ed. London: Routledge, 2013.

————."Being and Value. Thoughts on the Reform of the Metaphysics of Good within Value Philosophy." In *Aletheia* I, 2: 1977. (German and English.)

————. "Bonaventuras Interpretation der augustinischen These vom notwendigen Sein der Wahrheit," *Franziskanische Studien* 59 (1977), pp. 38-52.

————. "Can Neurological Evidence Refute Free Will? The Failure of a Phenomenological Analysis of Acts in Libet's Denial of 'Positive Free Will'." *Pensamiento. Revista de investigación e información filosófica*, vol. 67, núm. 254, *Ciencia, filosofía y religion. Serie especial no 5* (2011). pp. 1077-1098.

————. "Das Unsterblichkeitsproblem aus der Sicht der philosophischen Ethik und Anthropologie." *Franziskanische Studien*, H 3, 1978.

————. "Die verschiedenen Bedeutungen von 'Sein'." In *Wahrheit, Wert und Sein*. Balduin Schwarz, ed. pp. 301-332.

————. "Dietrich von Hildebrand on Benevolence in Love and Friendship: A Masterful Contribution to Perennial Philosophy," in *Journal of Philosophical Inquiry and Discussion: Selected Papers on the Philosophy of Dietrich von Hildebrand, Quaestiones Disputatae* 3, no. 2. Spring 2013, pp 85–106. Audio/video registration: http://www.hildebrandlegacy.org/main.cfm?r1=7.50&r2=1.00&r3=1.00&r4=0.00&id=109&level=3.

————. "Dietrich von Hildebrands philosophische Entdeckung der 'Wertantwort' und die Grundlegung der Ethik," in *Aletheia. An International Yearbook of Philosophy*, Volume V: *Truth and Value. The Philosophy of Dietrich von Hildebrand*, Josef Seifert ed. Bern: Peter Lang, 1992, pp. 34-58

————. *Discours des Méthodes. The Methods of Philosophy and Realist Phenomenology*. Frankfurt, 2009.

————."Duns Scotus' Philosophie des Individuums und Kritik am Abstraktionismus der aristotelischen Erkenntnistheorie als grandioses Beispiel einer mit dem christlichen Glauben vereinbaren Philosophie." *Intus legere. Filosofía* Vol. 9, No 2 (2015), pp 111-124.

————. *Erkenntnis objektiver Wahrheit*. Salzburg, 1972.

————. *Erkenntnis des Vollkommenen. Wege der Vernunft zu Gott*. Bonn: Lepanto Verlag, 2010. Also available in Spanish: *Conocimiento de Dios por las vías de la razón y del amor.* Pedro Jesús Teruel, trans. Revised and augmented by the author. Madrid: Encuentro, 2013.

―――. *Essere e persona. Verso una fondazione fenomenologica di una metafisica classica e personalistica.* Milan, 1989.

―――."Grundhaltung, Tugend und Handlung als ein Grundproblem der Ethik. Würdigung der Entdeckung der sittlichen Grundhaltung durch Dietrich von Hildebrand und kritische Untersuchung der Lehre von der 'Fundamentaloption' innerhalb der 'rein teleologischen' Begründung der Ethik." In *Ethik der Tugenden. Menschliche Grundhaltungen als unverzichtbarer Bestandteil moralischen Handelns. Festschrift für Joachim Piegsa zum 70. Geburtstag.* Clemens Breuer, ed. St. Ottilien: EOS Verlag, 2000. pp 311-360.

―――. *Heitere Philosophie — Philosophieren mit Johann Nestroy, dem witzigsten österreichischen Philosophen.* Mainz: Patrimonium-Verlag, 2016.

―――. "In Defense of Free Will: A Critique of Benjamin Libet." *Review of Metaphysics*, Vol. 65 (December 2011). pp. 377-407

―――. *Leib und Seele.* Salzburg, 1974.

―――. "Karol Cardinal Wojtyła (Pope John Paul II) as Philosopher and the Cracow/Lublin School of Philosophy." In *Aletheia* II (1981). pp. 130-199.

―――. "Moral Goodness Alone Is 'Good Without Qualifications': A Phenomenological Interpretation and Critical Development of some Kantian and Platonic Ethical Insights into Moral Facts which

Contribute to the Moral Education of Humanity." In *The Paideia Project* (20th World Congress of Philosophy in Boston August 10-15, 1998) http://www.bu.edu/wcp/Papers/TEth/TEthSeif.htm.

————. "Ontic and Moral Goods and Evils. On the Use and Abuse of Important Ethical Distinctions." *Anthropotes* 2. Rome, 1987.

————. "Persons and Causes: beyond Aristotle." *Journal of East-West Thought*. Fall Issue Nr. 3, Vol. 2 (September 2012): 1-32.

————. "Persons, Causes and Free Will: Libet's Topsy-Turvy Idea of the Order of Causes and 'Forgetfulness of the Person'." *Journal of East-West Thought*. Summer Nr. 2 Vol. 4, (June 2014): 13-51.

————. "Philosophizing with Plato about the Immortality of the Soul." *Philosophical News*. No. 8, March 2014. *Anima*, pp. 140-162.

————. "¿Poseemos y somos un alma inmortal?" *Philosophia* 73, 1 (2013). pp. 13-42.

————. "¿Tenemos y somos un alma espiritual e inmortal?" in Carlos Casanova (ed.), Josef Seifert, and Daniel von Wachter. *El alma, la providencia y el derecho natural (un ejercicio de filosofía como capacidad de juzgar)*: conferencia de cierre de la International Academy of Philosophy at the Pontificia Universidad Católica de CHILE (2015). pp. 11-40.

————. "The Problem of the Moral Significance of Human Fertility and Birth Control Methods. Philosophical Arguments against Contraception?" in *Humanae Vitae: 20 Anni Dopo*, Acts of the Second

International Congress of Moral Theology, Rome, 1988, pp. 661-672.

————. "Una reflexion filosófica y una defensa de *Humanae Vitae*. El don del amor y de la nueva vida," in: Benedicto XVI, Karol Wojtyła, Carlo Caffarra, Antonio Mᵉ Rouco Varela, Angelo Scola, Livio Melina, Alfonso López Trujillo, Fernando Chomali, Josef Seifert, *A cuarenta años de la Encíclica Humanae Vitae, Cuaderno Humanitas* ⁻ No 19, Pontificia Universidad Católica de Chile, Octubre 2008, pp. 49-59.

————. "The Splendor of Truth and Intrinsically Immoral Acts I: A Philosophical Defense of the Rejection of Proportionalism and Consequentialism in Veritatis Splendor." *Studia philosophiae christianae* UKSW 51 (2015) 2, pp. 27-67.

————. "The Splendor of Truth and Intrinsically Immoral Acts II: A Philosophical Defense of the Rejection of Proportionalism and Consequentialism in Veritatis Splendor." *Studia Philosophiae Christianae* UKSW 51 (2015) 3, pp. 7-37.

————. *The Philosophical Diseases of Medicine and Their Cure. Philosophy and Ethics of Medicine.* Vol. 1: Foundations. Philosophy and Medicine, vol. 82. New York, 2004. Also, since 2005, available as Kluwer e-book.

————. "To Be a Person — To Be Free." In *Freedom in Contemporary Culture*, pp. 145-185. Zofia J. Zdybicka et al, eds. *Acts of the 5th World Congress of Christian Philosophy.* Catholic University of Lublin 20-25 August 1996, Vol I. Lublin: The University Press of the Catholic University of Lublin, 1998.

————. *True Love*. South Bend: St. Augustine Press, 2015.

————. "Verdad, Libertad y Amor en el Pensiamento Antropologico y Etico de Karol Wojtyła." In *Persona y Derecho*. Navarra, 1983. pp 177-193. Also published in *Veritas II*. Monterrey: Universidad Regiomontana, 1983.

————. *What is Life? On the Originality, Irreducibility and Value of Life*. Value Inquiry Book Series (VIBS). Robert Ginsberg, ed. Vol. 51/Central European Value Studies (CEVS). H. G. Callaway, ed. Amsterdam, 1997.

————. "Wert und Wertantwort. Hildebrands Beitrag zur Ethik," in *Prima Philosophia*, Sonderheft 1, 1990.

Spaemann, Robert. *Spontaneität und Reflexion*. Stuttgart, 1968.

Thomas Aquinas. *Summa Theologiae*. Prima Secundae. 3d edition. Matriti, 1962.

————. *De Veritate*. Roma, 1952.

Waldstein, Wolfgang. *Vorpositive Ordnungselemente im römischen Recht. Salzburger Universitätsreden*, Heft 19. Salzburg, 1967.

Wenisch, Bernhard. *Der Wert. Eine an D. v. Hildebrand orientierte Auseinandersetzung mit Max Scheler*. Unpublished dissertation. Salzburg, 1968.

Wenisch, Fritz. *Die Objektivität der Werte*. Regensburg, 1971.

————. *Die Philosophie und ihre Methode*. Salzburg: A. Pustet, 1976.

INDEX

method, 3, 4, 5

Mill, John Stuart, 13, 130

Moore, G. E., 13, 17, 34, 130

moral action, 4, 7, 8, 17, 18, 21, 25,
29, 30, 33, 36, 38, 39, 40, 41, 45,
46, 47, 50, 52, 54, 55, 59, 60, 63,
64, 65, 66, 67, 71, 72, 73, 76, 78,
79, 80, 82, 85, 86, 87, 88, 92, 93,
95, 96, 97, 98, 99, 101, 102, 103,
105, 106, 107, 108, 110, 113, 116,
117, 118, 120, 121, 123, 124, 126,
127, 128

moral actions, 8, 16, 17, 18, 20, 30,
36, 48, 57, 60, 71, 72, 73, 81, 87,
89, 93, 99, 114, 120

moral duties, 42, 84

moral obligations, 50, 61, 68, 72, 97,
98

moral value, 13, 19, 33, 34, 35, 38,
39, 53, 54, 55, 57, 65, 66, 76, 78,
81, 84, 86, 88, 89, 90, 92, 93, 95,
96, 98, 99, 106, 107, 108, 110

moral values, 2, 17, 18, 36, 37, 38, 43,
45, 53, 57, 59, 73, 76, 83, 89, 90,
91, 92, 98, 124

morality, 17, 18, 20, 25, 27, 32, 35,
37, 38, 42, 46, 50, 51, 70, 76, 82,
83, 84, 88, 92, 96, 98, 100, 105,
108, 112, 113, 114, 115, 116, 119,
120, 123, 125, 126

morally good action, 17, 21, 23, 32,
95, 96, 113

morally obligatory (action), 17, 19,
20, 21, 55, 62, 68, 76, 80, 82, 102,
108, 117, 119, 122, 126

motive, 7, 8, 22, 24, 26, 27, 28, 38, 39,
40, 44, 45, 49, 60, 63, 64, 66, 71,
78, 80, 88, 92, 93, 95, 102, 103,
106, 107, 108, 110, 113, 116, 118,
121, 123, 126

necessitating, 20

Newman, John Henry, 105, 131

obedience, 12, 71, 78, 82, 83, 84, 103,

110

objective, 5, 7, 8, 22, 23, 25, 27, 34,
40, 45, 49, 50, 53, 55, 65, 69, 84,
91, 103, 116

obligation, 19, 21, 24, 34, 43, 50, 51,
54, 60, 64, 65, 66, 67, 68, 69, 71,
72, 73, 75, 76, 77, 78, 80, 82, 86,
87, 93, 96, 98, 99, 101, 103, 104,
105, 108, 115, 117, 119, 121, 125

obligatory, 18, 20, 21, 26, 55, 59, 73,
78, 81, 122

Ockham, William of, 126

ought, 4, 5, 18, 26, 34, 43, 61, 78, 82,
87, 92, 103, 112, 117, 118, 123

Paton, Herbert James, 31, 49, 130

Paul the Apostle, 90, 91, 105

person, 18, 21, 22, 23, 26, 28, 37, 41,
44, 51, 55, 57, 58, 59, 61, 63, 66,
67, 68, 69, 71, 72, 74, 76, 77, 78,
81, 82, 83, 86, 87, 88, 96, 97, 98,
99, 101, 104, 105, 114, 115, 117,
118, 124, 125

Pfänder, Alexander, 3, 22, 28, 131

Pharisaic, 57, 66, 88, 90

Pharisaism, 57, 89, 90

Piegsa, Joachim, 14, 134

Plato, 2, 3, 15, 16, 40, 47, 90, 106,
112, 125, 131, 135

positive command, 69, 73

practical principle, 49, 50

Premm, Matthias, 45

Principia Ethica, 13, 34, 130

priority, 80, 82, 93

promise, 69, 70, 73, 113

psychological, 4, 5, 8, 93, 94

Rahner, Karl, 107

realizable through me, 12, 14

reason, 10, 22, 24, 26, 27, 35, 41, 49,
50, 58, 66, 70, 80, 105, 122

Reinach, Adolf, 3, 69, 131

Reiner, Hans, 51, 52, 131

relativism, 68

rights, ii, 50, 54

ABOUT THE AUTHOR

Josef Seifert, b. 1945. Ph.D. in philosophy 1969; Habilitation at the University of Munich 1975. Assistant Professor at the University of Salzburg, Associate Professor at the University of Dallas; at the International Academy of Philosophy (IAP) in Texas and Founding Rector and Full Professor of the IAP Liechtenstein (1986-); Full Professor at the IAP-PUC in Chile (2004-2012); Dietrich von Hildebrand Chair for Realist Phenomenology at the IAP-IFES), Granada, Spain (2011-). Author of 29 philosophical books in German, English, Italian, and Spanish (many of them translated into other languages), and 360 articles in 12 languages. His published books and articles deal with questions of epistemology, logic and theory of truth, methodology, game theory, philosophy of medicine and science, ontology, metaphysics, philosophy of God, philosophical anthropology (body-mind problem, life, death, genders, love and marriage, homosexuality, "brain-death"), ethics, aesthetics, philosophy of religion. He is considered by many to be the leading representative of realist phenomenological philosophy today. His best known works include *Erkenntnis objektiver Wahrheit* (Knowledge of Objective Truth. The Transcendence of Man in Knowledge); *Leib und Seele.* (Body and Soul. A Contribution towards a Philosophical Anthropology); *Das Leib-Seele Problem und die gegenwärtige philosophische Diskussion.* (The Body/Mind Problem and the Contemporary Philosophical Discussion. A Critical and Systematic Investigation); *Back to Things in Themselves. A Phenomenological Foundation for Classical Realism; Being and Person. Towards a Phenomenological Foundation of a Classical and Personalistic Metaphysics* (Itaian 1989, enlaged English edition 2016); *Schachphilosophie; Sein und Wesen/Being and Essence* (1996); *Gott als Gottesbeweis. Eine phänomenologische Neubegründung des ontologischen Arguments/* God as Proof of His Own Existence. A New Phenomenological Foundation of the Ontological Argument

(2000; 2001 in Arabic; 2004 in Rumanian); *What is Life? The Originality, Irreducibility, and Value of Life*; *Ritornare a Platone. La fenomenlogia realista come riforma critica della dottrina platonica delle idee.* In the Appendix an unedited work by Adolf Reinach on Plato; *Superación del escándalo de la razón pura. La ausencia de contradicción de la realidad, a pesar de Kant*; *Philosophical Diseases of Medicine and Their Cure.* Philosophy and Ethics of Medicine. Vol. 1.; *Wahrheit und Person* / Truth and Person. On the Essence of the Truth of Being, of Knowledge, and of the Judgment; *Der Streit um die Wahrheit. (The Controversy about Truth. Truth and Truth Theories)*; *Discours des Méthodes. The Methods of Philosophy and Realist Phenomenology*; *Conocimiento de Dios por las vías de la razón y del amor*; *True Love.* Of his articles "Philosophy as a Rigorous Science. Towards the Foundations of a Realist Phenomenological Method – in Critical Dialogue with Edmund Husserl's Ideas about Philosophy as a Rigorous Science" (in German and Czech 1996, in Russian 1997, in in Lithuanian 1988, in Italian 2001); "Is 'Brain Death' actually Death?" *The Monist 76* (1993); "The Idea of the Good as the Sum-total of Pure Perfections. A New Personalistic Reading of Republic VI and VII" (2002); "Absolute Moral Obligations towards Finite Goods as Foundation of Intrinsically Right and Wrong Actions. A Critique of Consequentialist 'Teleological Ethics': Destruction of Ethics through Moral Philosophy?" (1985); "Is the Right to Life or is another Right the most Fundamental Human Right - das 'Urgrundrecht'? Human Dignity, Moral Obligations, Natural Rights, and Positive Rights?"(2013).

Honors and distinctions include: Honorary Member of the Medical Faculty of the Pontifical Catholic University of Chile in Santiago (since 1993); Recipient of EU (European Community) Medal of Merit and Recipient of the EU Order of Merit; "Austrian Cross of Merit for Science and Art 1st Class"; Dr. honoris causa.

Under the pen-name Melchior B. author of 5 published short stories and author of a novel (not yet published).

Made in the USA
Monee, IL
08 July 2022

99291370R00085